A Theory of Republican Character

and Related Essays

A Theory of Republican Character and Related Essays

Wendell John Coats, Jr.

SUP

Selinsgrove: Susquehanna University Press
London and Toronto: Associated University Presses

Associated University Presses
440 Forsgate Drive
Cranbury, NJ 08512

Associated University Presses
25 Sicilian Avenue
London WC1A 2QH, England

Associated University Presses
P.O. Box 338, Port Credit
Mississauga, Ontario
Canada L5G 4L8

The paper used in this publication meets the requirements of the American National Standard for Permanence of Paper for Printed Library Materials Z39.48-1984.

Library of Congress Cataloging-in-Publication Data

Coats, Wendell John.
A theory of republican character and related essays / Wendell John Coats, Jr.
p. cm.
Includes bibliographical references and index.
ISBN 0-945636-58-X (alk. paper)
1. Republicanism. 2. Republics. 3. Democracy. 4. Political science—History. I. Title.
JC423.C644 1994
321.8—dc20 92-51005
CIP

PRINTED IN THE UNITED STATES OF AMERICA

For Karen Ann
and Karen Evangeline

Contents

Introduction 9

1. A Theory of Republican Character—For a Democratic Age 15
2. Some Correspondences Between Oakeshott's "Civil Condition" and the Republican Tradition 63
3. American Democracy and the Punitive Use of Force: Requiem for the McNamara Model 78
4. Drama and Democracy 119

Epilogue 144

Appendix A. Two Views of Aristotle's *Politics* 147

Appendix B. Review of *The Voice of Liberal Learning: Michael Oakeshott on Education* 158

Index 165

Introduction

> The subdivision of the arts and professions, in certain examples, tends to improve them. . . . But to separate the arts which form the citizen and the statesman, the arts of policy and war, is an attempt to dismember the human character, and to destroy the very arts we mean to improve.
>
> —Adam Ferguson, *Essay on the History of Civil Society*

The title essay of this book attempts to give an account of what I call the "republican character," to distinguish it from its democratic sibling, and to do so in such a way as to make it intelligible for a modern, largely democratic audience. That this distinction be made intelligible to the democratic personality is important, I shall argue, because the issue is not merely an academic one. It has important long-range constitutional and political implications as well.

The basis for the distinction between these two forms of constitutions and their corresponding characters is to be found in Aristotle's account of even the highest form of democracy (agrarian), as perverted since it is not directed toward the "common advantage";[1] and in his account of the regime mixed of democracy and oligarchy sustained by middling citizens capable of serving as heavy infantry in defense of their city, as being the lowest constitutional form capable of achieving the common good or advantage.[2] This essay begins with this distinction from Aristotle's *Politics*, and tries to find both conscious and implicit support for it in the writings of various theorists across two millennia, for example, Cicero, Machiavelli, de Tocqueville, James Harrington, and James Madison; it also looks at the views of critics of this distinction such as Woodrow Wilson and FDR. And it turns to a recent Supreme Court case in an attempt to illustrate, in the opposing judgments of various justices, the existence, side by side, of both the republican and democratic characters in the contemporary body politic of the United States.

Since the essay is written for a democratic audience in a democratic age, and since I am arguing that democracy tends to psychologize and otherwise reduce its political abstractions in the overriding interest of personal happiness, I have cast the argument in terms of republican and democratic characters, rather than in terms of regimes or constitutions. Also, since I am primarily concerned with the differences between the lowest form of the Aristotelian republic and the various stages of democracy (as reflected in the respective characters they nourish), I have tried to downplay the differences between ancient and modern republicanism.[3]

The second essay is entitled, "Some Correspondences Between Michael Oakeshott's 'Civil Condition' and the Republican Tradition." It highlights affinities between republicanism and Oakeshott's classical liberalism, and was written for the 1992 volume of *The Political Science Reviewer* dedicated to his work. I include it here because it can be read as an expansion of the first essay's discussion of republicanism, classical liberalism, and welfare liberalism, and serves to illustrate in added ways what is different and troubling about the "democratic personality."

The third piece, "American Democracy and the Punitive Use of Force: Requiem for the McNamara Model," was written under a 1989 grant from the U.S. Institute of Peace in Washington, D.C. It starts with an analysis of an essentially economic paradigm (the "McNamara model") for the threat and use of force in the nuclear age, and tries to demonstrate the ways in which it had pervaded all of U.S. thinking and policy concerning the use of force over the past thirty years, down to guerrilla and "low-intensity" operations. The monograph's conclusion tries to show how the attempt to reduce the use of even nonnuclear force to an economic activity of "coercive diplomacy," is consistent with Plato's prediction about the evolution of democracies. The article is a continuation of some of my previous work on the subject.[4] A somewhat altered and shortened version of it (less the Platonic conclusions), was published in the Fall 1989 issue of *Strategic Review*, a defense policy journal with prominent military and political leaders among its subscribers. (To judge from the conduct of the military operations in the 1991 war against Iraq, the U.S. military would seem to have freed themselves from the "economic" view of warfare that characterized the Vietnam War,[5] though it is difficult to generalize on the basis of the Gulf War since it had so many unique, political aspects.) I include the monograph in this collection because it articulates in some detail, a conception of the common defense as intended first and foremost to preserve a system of political authority (rather than bargain over increments of pain inflicted or threatened), an outlook essential for the continued viability of the "republican character."

The fourth essay, "Drama and Democracy," was written expressly for this collection. It attempts to illustrate—through an analysis of seven plays—how drama may be used pedagogically to resist the reductivist and "homogenizing" tendencies of both the modern scientific method and modern democracy. The essay's central idea is that, in contrast to the method of scientific generalization—classifying phenomena (including human phenomena) as functions of a presupposed unity of variables—both political philosophy and drama tend to accept the idea of human society as an ordered whole whose unity is achieved in the integration of both likes and unlikes.

In addition to a brief Epilogue summarizing the volume's major themes, I have included as Appendexes, two short pieces. One, "Two Views of Aristotle's *Politics*," was delivered as an address to the International Studies Forum at Connecticut College. I think it is relevant to this collection because it attempts to illustrate in dramatic detail some problems with the argument (of some modern historians) that observations of Aristotle can hardly be of relevance today. The second piece is a book review of *The Voice of Liberal Learning: Michael Oakeshott on Education*, edited by Timothy Fuller. It was originally written at the request of an education journal editor who subsequently decided that it was "too philosophical" for her readers. I include it here because Oakeshott's view of meaning and teaching in the liberal arts is characteristic, in its cultivation of the practice of comprehensive, individual judgment, of what I have called the "republican generalist" within modern, liberal democracy.

My thanks to Connecticut College, The Earhart Foundation, and the U.S. Institute of Peace, for support during the research and writing of these essays; to the National Endowment for the Humanities for a summer seminar at Princeton University with Prof. Alan Ryan which afforded me the opportunity to study the works of the "republican" theorist, James Harrington; to the chapter of the Conference for the Study of Political Thought at Kenyon College, Gambier, Ohio for listening to and commenting on a draft of the title essay; and to colleagues and friends who were kind enough to read and make suggestions on various essays—Dick Birdsall, Wendell Coats, Sr., Ed Cranz, Tim Fuller,

Dirk Held, Pamela Jensen, Maureen Moakely, and Leslie Rubin, among others.

Notes

1. Aristotle *Politics* 4, 4; 6, 1–5.
2. Aristotle *Politics* 4, 8–11.
3. See, in this connection, the sections on Montesquieu and *The Federalist* in the title essay, "A Theory of Republican Character—For a Democratic Age."
4. Most of this work is collected in my book, *The Activity of Politics and Related Essays* (Selinsgrove, Pa.: Susquehanna University Press, 1989).
5. The Gulf War was a limited war in the sense that the Korean (but not the Vietnam) War was limited. That is, the application of force was limited by political decisions at the highest level, rather than through the attempted mutation of military concepts at the operational and tactical levels by civilian administrators and academics. For a similar view of the Gulf War, see the editorial by Mackubin Owens, "Desert Storm and the Renaissance in Military Doctrine," *Strategic Review* 19, no. 2 (Spring 1991), especially 6. "The U.S. military victory was above all a victory for doctrine developed and tested within the Services."

A Theory of Republican Character

and Related Essays

1
A Theory of Republican Character— For a Democratic Age

> Some of men's wrong actions are referred by Chrysippus to . . . the soul's lack of tension and its weakness. . . . He says there are times when we give up right decisions because the soul's tension gives in. . . .
>
> —Galen *Stoicorum Veterum Fragmenta* 3–473

Introduction

The aim of this essay is to establish significant differences between what I call the "republican" and "democratic" characters, both as an aid to our own self-understanding, and, perhaps (unfortunately) as an extended epitaph for the former. This is a distinction that democracies must understand, in light of the long-observed tendency of advanced or old democracies to render their political and civil vocabularies superfluous by reducing them in use to subpolitical (especially economic and lower psychic) dimensions.[1]

I focus on the issue of character, by which I mean, a pattern of fairly settled perspectives, habits, and characteristics in individuals, itself the outcome of some combination of upbringing, education, experience, and self-motivation. I do so out of the belief that democracy can only resist its "subpolitical" tendencies if there are some republican characters left around to exert influence; out of the observation that democracy—in its fixation on personal happiness—is more inclined to listen to discussions of personality and psychology than to ones about constitutional forms; and out of the observation that the residual republican characteristics in the Constitution of the United States, in particular, have been largely circumvented by technological innovations and legal interpretations.

The republican character, as I understand it, may be *initially* specified as follows: that character that automatically readjusts itself whenever it knows that it has taken personal and private interest and expression beyond the point that it can any longer care for the common or general good—that is, any longer still be properly thought of as "political."[2] (And if its profession is one of governmental or military service, it is incapable of viewing its work as merely a source of income for private pursuits, a disposition evident in its willingness to make sacrifice incommensurate with its pecuniary remuneration.) By contrast, the democrat may be initially specified as similar to the dweller in a huge metropolis who puts great energy into mastering a nonpolitical and urbane specialty or profession,[3] and feels instinctively, that it would be grotesquely amateurish to attempt a competent grasp of the public business (including even his own self-defense). I believe both of these characters are recognizable on today's political landscape, though the latter is more clearly in abundance.

The distinction I see between these two characters (and their respective constitutional forms) has always been elusive, but there have always been some theorists who saw it, for example, Aristotle, Thucydides, James Harrington, and James Madison; and others who shed light on the distinction even when uninterested in the particular issue, for example, Plato, Cicero, Machiavelli, Montesquieu, Rousseau, and de Tocqueville. (And, still others, who recognized the distinction within popular forms of government and character, but obscured it—Woodrow Wilson, for example.)

I propose to look at the insights of these and other writers as a preface to specifying the more detailed differences which I see between these two characters or personae across Western political history and reflection. Obviously I believe there are insights of Aristotle and Cicero which can be relevant for us,[4] if phrased generally enough, if for no other reason than that the theorists and founders of political modernity (and medievalism) were influenced by them. I shall especially be taking my bearings from Aristotle's distinction between even the highest form of democracy (agrarian—which he still thought partial or unfocused on the common advantage), and the lowest constitutional form (polity or republic) still devoted to the common advantage, one sustained by "middling" citizens capable of alternating rule over one another, and of serving as heavy armed infantry in defense of their city. Aristotle thought and wrote within a civilization which, like our own, had a long and differentiated experience with popular government, and he provides a good point of departure for distinguishing between republics and democracies, and the respective characters they nourish.

Before taking up Aristotle's observations on the differences between democracies and republics (polities), a few words are in order about the selection of theorists and writers in the discussions which follow. My general aim here is to search for support and illumination in the history of Western political thought for the distinction between the republican and democratic character. Most of the authors I take up were interested in constitutional forms rather than character (with the exception of Aristotle, who discusses both in the *Politics* and the *Ethics*, respectively); many have no distinction between republican and democratic; they often use the word *republic* in very different senses; and they write in different historical contexts (though often explictly addressing one another across the ages, ignorant of the modern historical claim that they were thereby being irrelevant to their own time). Nevertheless, I forge ahead, bringing in any of their insights which shed light on this elusive distinction, before attempting my own formulation midway in the essay. And I cite these various authors not in an ambitious attempt to prove the existence of some sort of continuous republican tradition across the ages, but from the conviction that advanced democracy is more of a "psychological" than a narrowly political or constitutional phenomenon, and should evince certain fundamental similarities in individuals any time that it occurs. Hence, one way of establishing some commonality among various republicanisms, is to show what they are *not*, that is, how they resist and differ from the characteristics of advanced democracy. In the hope of maintaining interest for both the political theorist and the concerned generalist, I have addressed some issues of scholarly dispute, but relegated them to the Notes.

Aristotle

Crucial to our discussion here is Aristotle's distinction in the *Politics* between the highest form of democracy and the lowest form of polity (or "constitutional government"). Democracy, for Aristotle, was a perverted form of rule since it aimed primarily at the good of a class—the many, or freeborn, or poor—rather than at the good of the whole body politic.[5] But the best mix of democracy and oligarchy which he called by the generic name, "polity," was distinguished by the existence and support of a middle class interested in the common advantage. The interesting question for our analysis becomes the essential difference between his highest form of democracy—that by farmers residing in the county and coming to town to vote—and the polity or middle-class regime of laws directed toward mediation of the class conflicts of perverted regimes—democracy, oligarchy, and tyranny.

Where does concern for the "common advantage" begin to arise in Aristotle's view? What distinguishes the citizen of the polity from the agrarian democrats who are "good"[6] only in the negative sense that since they value farming over politics, and live in the country, they are inclined to live by (class-oriented) laws rather than diurnal decrees, and are not inclined to use political office for personal gain. Aristotle's reasoning here in several passages of the *Politics* is unambiguous. He traces the origins of the concern for the common advantage in the *majority* of people to tactically coordinated military capabilities in defense of the city. To say this differently, Aristotle traces the generic political constitution (polity or republic) to the evolution of tactically skilled, heavy-armed infantry, arising from the middling classes (those with sufficient property to own heavy arms and armor), capable of repelling the attacks of both oligarchic cavalry, and mobile, lightly armed democratic forces, that is, capable of preserving the middle-class regime which cooperates through moderate politics. ("For those who have authority over arms also have authority over whether the regime will last or not."[7])

Let us follow Aristotle's reasoning as illustrated in various observations from the *Politics*.

> When the multitude governs with a view to the common advantage, it is called by the term common to all regimes, polity.[8]

> Military virtue . . . arises in a multitude; hence in this regime the warrior element is the most authoritative, and it is those possessing (heavy) arms who share in it.[9]

> A polity should be made up only of those possessing (heavy) arms . . . (or) of those who had once done so.[10]

> Without organization the heavy-armed element is useless. . . . But as cities increased in size and those with (heavy) arms provided relatively more strength, more persons shared in the regime. *Hence the*

regimes we now call polities used to be called democracies.[11] (Emphasis added.)

Now, Aristotle certainly observes other characteristics in this middling character—it is open to reason, capable of liberality, and possesses a stability deriving from its proximity to, and experience of, all other classes, the rich, the poor, and the powerful.[12] But Aristotle's implication is clear in the passages cited, that the specific excellence of the middling classes he observed is the capacity to function cooperatively as heavy-armed infantry in defense of the city; and that it is through this excellence that they learn to care for the common advantage; to rule and be ruled by one another; and to live in a regime of laws dispensing political justice understood as rewards commensurate with contributions to the common advantage.[13]

In the *Nicomachean Ethics,* Aristotle gives additional insight into the character of this middling regime. He says here that the relationship obtaining among citizens of different constitutional forms can be illustrated by analogy with forms of friendship; and that the relationship of this middling constitution is like that among brothers.

> The ideal . . . is that all citizens shall be equal and shall be good, so that they all rule in turn, and all have an equal share of power; and therefore the friendship between them is also one of equality.[14]

Aristotle also distinguishes this relationship from that among citizens of democracy, by saying that while democracy is only a small deviation from the constitutional form of government, it differs in that its equality ressembles not that among brothers (who are truly equal in status and outlook), but that among the members of an entire household where "the ruler of the house is weak, and everyone is allowed to do what he likes."[15]

Thucydides

Thucydides is worth citing in this discussion for his reference to a brief Athenian regime of five thousand citizens, in the *History of the Peloponnesian Wars,* which he viewed as neither oligarchic nor democratic. He says that power was handed over to those with sufficient property to provide themselves with the equipment of a heavy-armed infantryman (hoplite). Here is what Thucydides says of this regime which he viewed from exile:

> Indeed, during the first period of this new regime the Athenians appear to have had a better government than ever before, at least in my time. There was a reasonable and moderate blending of the few and the many. . . .[16]

There has been much discussion of this paragraph among classical scholars, with modern partisans of democracy tending to dismiss it out of hand as simply oligarchic prejudice, or even "sour grapes."[17] Yet Thucydides prided himself on seeing clearly and telling things as they were, and this paragraph is interesting as an instance of a view before Aristotle describing an "intermediate regime" of middling citizens capable of providing for the common defense, which was neither oligarchy nor democracy, and which was characterized by its balance. This is also the view of at least some modern classics scholars as well.

> The assembly must have been once more the controlling body in the state, and the theory that it was an assembly limited to hoplites remains the best explanation of the difference between the intermediate regime and the democracy.[18]

Polybius and Cicero

What can be learned from Polybius and Cicero about the differences between the republican and democratic characters is meager and must be obtained obliquely, since neither was expressly concerned with the distinction which Aristotle introduced, and as is well-known, Polybius even changed Aristotle's taxonomy of regimes to call democracy the good form of popular government.[19]

The most interesting idea for our analysis is what Cicero understood the Romans of the republic to mean by *respublica* and "keeping faith," and fulfilling one's obligations in that context. Consider the following assorted observations from Cicero's *De Officiis,* which convey the idea of a firm commitment to a rather complex and general set of civic obligations grounded in the distinction between what is public and what is private:

> The foundation of justice, moreover, is good faith—that is truth and fidelity to promises and agreements.[20]

> An oath is an assurance backed by religious sanctity; and a solemn

promise given . . . is to be sacredly kept. For the question . . . concerns . . . the obligations of justice and good faith.[21]

This, then, ought to be the chief end of all men, to make the interest of each individual and of the whole body politic identical. For, if the individual appropriates to selfish ends what should be the common good, all human fellowship will be destroyed.[22]

For . . . it is the peculiar function of the state and the city to guarantee to everyman the free and undisturbed control of his own particular property. . . . For the chief purpose in the establishment of the constitutional state . . . was that individual property rights might be secured.[23]

And, on the role of oaths among the Romans, here is Polybius in the sixth book of *The Histories:*

But the quality in which the Roman commonwealth is most distinctly superior is . . . the nature of their religious convictions . . . which maintains the cohesion of the Roman state . . . among the Romans those . . . dealing with large sums of money maintain correct conduct just because they have pledged their faith by oath.[24]

The insight I take from Cicero and Polybius is that the Roman idea of a republic was essentially a pledge or commitment to maintain a general distinction between what is public and private, and to protect and preserve the Roman way of life from foreign and domestic threats. The point for our analysis is that a "republic" was seen as a trust to preserve a general context within which public and private pursuits could occur, not an expectation of particular benefits. As a contemporary historian has written, "*Respublica* was . . . less a description of a specific form of government, than a pledge. . . . It stood above all else for the rule of the law. . . ."[25] And, in the same context, a contemporary English political theorist has rehabilitated the word *respublica* (in his own account of civil association) to mean

a practice of civility, specifying not performances but conditions to be subscribed to in choosing performances, and therefore the common or "public" concern. . . .[26]

Machiavelli

Machiavelli's reflections on the Roman republic in the *Discourses on Livy* and *The Prince*, though not concerned with fine distinctions between republics and democracies, do shed light on our problem. Some of Machiavelli's observations simply parallel those of Aristotle on the polity—it is a regime living under laws directed to the general good, constituted in conditions of relative equality, and supported by citizen armies. But it is Machiaveli's single-mindedness about overcoming the corruptions of time that leads to his new and systematic generalizations about republics. Throughout his political writings, Machiavelli, in effect, poses the question: If you would overcome (for so long as is ordained for you) the vicissitudes and corruptions of Fortune, solve for X and apply the results. X turns out to be a republic, understood as Machiavelli understood it, drawing upon observations about the Roman republic, owing to its success and longevity. Machiavelli was clearly a systematic thinker, and most of his maxims flow from this way of posing the problem of rule: "Assume as your highest goal the preservation of your state, at any cost;[27] then learn and imitate the characteristics of the most durable regime, the Roman republic."[28]

Five of Machiavelli's observations about the Roman republic will become important in our analysis of the republican character. Machiavelli thought that Rome's vitality derived from (1) the conflict between the nobles and the people, and the institutionalization of that conflict in the (separated) powers of the republic[29] (distinguished from the Polybian view that the republic's durability derived from the mere specialization of governmental functions);[30] (2) the diversity of citizens[31] arising under its form of government, in contrast to principalities; (3) Rome's ability to *renew* itself through tradition (returning to first principles[32], and innovation (expansion[33] and incorporation[34]); (4) its habits of military discipline, desirable not merely for their own sake, but because of their resistance to decay, whether in the shock of battle, or in the luxury of peace;[35] and (5) its unflinching belief in the sacredness of its public realm of freedom.[36] To summarize, then, Machiavelli's view would appear to be that republics are desirable for their balance, understood as a manageable tension successfully combining tradition and innovation to master the vicissitudes of Fortune, for so long as it is given to a people to do so. (Machiavelli thought that we could fall from power before it was ordained by Fortune, through lack of skill, but not extend our time in power through use of skill; however, he did not think this consideration should affect us negatively, since we could never know in advance when our time was up, and, hence, should always strive to maintain power, that is, master Fortune for a while longer.)

James Harrington

The English civil war, utopian work, *The Commonwealth of Oceana*, by James Harrington, is interesting for several modifications he makes to Machiavelli's argument about Rome, and because of Harrington's subsequent influence in America, documented recently in J.G.A. Pocock's *Machiavellian Moment.* (David Hume remarked that Harrington was superior among utopians because he assumed "no reformation in the manners of men."[37]) Harrington refers to Machiavelli many times in *Oceana*, calls him a great artist, and corrects him occasionally, especially for not seeing the dangers to the Roman republic of a permanent and entrenched senate with too much property.[38] As Pocock has also noted in his long introduction to Harrington's collected works, Harrington's aim is to modify Machiavelli on the requirements for a republic which can withstand the corruptions of time.[39]

The amplification which Harrington makes to Machiavelli's requirement for an independent citizen army as the basis for republican freedom, concerns the economic conditions needed in order for this army to sustain itself. On Harrington's account, this involves an equal, agrarian land distribution scheme. But the point for our analysis is that the economic arrangements are simply a means for guaranteeing the material and moral autonomy of the citizens who comprise the citizen army. On this point, Pocock describes *Oceana* as a "civil history of the sword and property," and says of the book's subsequent influence:

> If the republican tradition had derived from Harrington the belief that commercial man was capable of the material and moral autonomy of the citizen, it had similarly derived the belief that the mode of property which best guaranteed autonomy and virtue was that which best guaranteed independence. . . .[40]

A second of Harrington's general points which will be useful for our theme, is his claim that while a lasting and stable regime must include the people as a component of democracy, it must include an aristocratic component as well, in this case a (nonhereditary) senate to formulate issues which the people would resolve. More generally stated, Harrington's commonwealth is based upon the idea of *deference* to natural political talent, which he appears to think will always be recognized without ambiguity.

> Twenty men . . . can never come together, but there will be such a difference in them that about a third will be wiser, or at least less foolish, than all the rest. These upon acquaintance . . . will be discovered and . . . lead. . . . Wherefore this can be no other than a natural aristocracy . . . such as the people have . . . a positive obligation to make use of as their guides. . . .[41]

As Pocock observes on this general point, "But Harrington was a republican—an aristocrat because he was a democrat; and on the democratic side of this thought he was nearly a Leveller."[42] (I have relied so heavily on Pocock's treatment of Harrington, that I should mention in passing that one shortcoming in it is not to establish more clearly that the emphasis of Harrington and Machiavelli before him on arms and political freedom is to be explicitly found in Aristotle's treatment of the polity or mixed regime.)

Rousseau

In the *Social Contract* Rousseau calls Machiavelli a profound political thinker, a good citizen, and a lover of republican liberty.[43] But does he add to Machiavelli's understanding of the longevity of the Roman republic as a tension between tradition and innovation; and to our own understanding of the differences between democracies and republics? If we put on one side Rousseau's romantic, "either-or" way of phrasing problems ("one must choose between making a man or a citizen"; "As soon as public service ceases to be the chief business of the citizen . . . the state is not far from its fall"),[44] I believe he does.

Rousseau was very interested in the problem of change and flux, and how to resist it.[45] His criticism of democracy is precisely that it is the most subject to internal agitation. "There is none which has so strong a tendency to change to another form. . . ."[46] And, in his account of the stability of the Roman republic he adds to Machiavelli's analysis of the conflict of orders, the tension between the rural or traditional and the urban, and the predominance of the former.

> The distinction between urban and rural tribes had one effect which

is worth mention, both because it is without parallel elsewhere, and because to it Rome owed the preservation of her morality. . . .[47]

And, on the same point:

Where is the modern people among whom . . . unrest, intrigue, continual removals, and perpetual changes . . . could let such a system last for twenty years without turning the state upside down.[48]

Although Rousseau's strong desire for psychic harmony would not allow him to suggest that Rome's longevity resided in the *tension* between the innovation of the city and the tradition of the countryside, he did highlight the blindness and folly of his contemporary cities in their fixation on change for its own sake by holding up to them less urbane and more admirable ancient alternatives grounded in agricultural and military prowess.

The taste of the early Romans for the country-side is well known. This taste they owed to their wise founder, who made rural and military labour go along with liberty, and, so to speak, relegated to the town arts, crafts, intrigue, fortune, and slavery.[49]

Before leaving the subject of Rousseau's "republicanism," it is interesting to refer to his account of the "general will" in order to show why it is *not* a feature of the republican character, but rather more accurately to be described as "aristocratic" in its requirement for a Spartan-like devotion to the common good. Readers of *The Social Contract* will recall that one of Rousseau's themes is the civic corruption which follows from the growth of particular interests over the general interest.

When particular interests begin to make themselves felt and smaller societies to exercise an influence over the larger, the common interest changes and finds opponents . . . the general will ceases to be the will of all. . . .[50]

Rousseau's corrective for this situation is a conception (in each citizen) of the state as arising from the alienation of each's own prepolitical prerogatives, to the state as a whole, understood in its uncorrupted form through an abstraction called "the general will." But by posing the alternatives in such Romantic, "either-or" terms ("is it to the advantage of the State?" or "of advantage to this or that man or party?"), Rousseau forgoes the ideal of the mixed or balanced character who, when he cannot reconcile them in a single view, puts private concern first in some cases, and public concern in other cases, based on his judgment about likely effects in the circumstances on public authority, fellow citizens, and his own self and kin. Unlike the citizen of *The Social Contract*, the republican character is moderately dependent upon others, and requires the art of politics for the moderate reconciliation of differences with them. Hence, there is some justice in the characterization of Rousseau as erring (in his account of the general will) in the direction of the "tyranny of the soul," rather than in the democratic direction of the "tryanny of the body."[51] (On the other hand, Rousseau's emphasis on *feelings* in the *Confessions* and elsewhere, would seem to fuel the democratic propensity for exaggerated care of the body and the lower psychic needs.)

Montesquieu

Mentioning Montesquieu is important here since his reading of the British Constitution in *The Spirit of the Laws* as preserving civic liberty while favoring commerce over philosophy and public service, has been interpreted to mean a modern form of republicanism which especially influenced the authors of the *Federalist* (although Montesquieu himself equated republicanism with a thing of the past based on ancient virtue[52]). This new republicanism is seen to differ from both the classical and the Renaissance humanist versions of republicanism in its preference for grounding personal and political liberty in enlightened self-interest and institutional arrangements, rather than in public-spiritedness and the civic education to make it pervasive and enduring.[53] There is certainly something to this claim if it is not stated too rigidly, but Montesquieu's main concern was to deflate the claims of monarchy as good and virtuous government, not to elucidate differences between greater and lesser degrees of republicanism and democracy. Hence, I leave to a discussion of the *Federalist,* whose authors claim to be both republican and in possession of a new political science, more detailed consideration of the content of the new republicanism and its affinity with older republicanism, and its differences with democracy.

The Federalist

If Rousseau may be said to have rescued some of the respectability of the virtue of ancient city-states from Montesquieu's apology for cosmopolitan commercialism, the *Federalist* authors (and the constitution they defend) may be seen as going out to meet and accommodate Montesquieu (and David Hume), while still viewing themselves as republican. What do they mean by the new republicanism, other than representative democracy? And how does it differ from ancient republics and democracies, besides the use of the elective principle representing the people as a whole?

The historian Forrest McDonald has identified two distinct patterns of American republicanism during the founding period.[54] One, which he calls "puritanical republicanism," emphasized private, moral rectitude as the basis for "public virtue," in turn as the solution to the mortality of republics.[55] The other, which is part of the Machiavellian-Harringtonian-country-whig inheritance, he calls the agrarian or "tobacco-plantation-country" version. This latter form of republicanism was characterized by a leisure ethic, personal independence, and military ability, and strict attention to institutional arrangements as the basis for political and personal liberty.[56] Above all, this *ethos* was characterized by the existence of a bond of understanding (similar to Ciceronian *fides*) among economically and militarily independent citizens. It is this second ethic, with its emphasis on personal independence as guaranteed by institutional arrangements, especially as transmitted through the pen of the Virginian, James Madison, which is more clearly evident in the pages of the *Federalist* and the constitution.

There are several aspects of *Federalist* republicanism which must be expressly delineated in order to show the contrast with subsequent, more democratic developments. First, there is clearly the Machiavellian outlook on political stability and longevity arising in the tension between the old and the new, between tradition and innovation. This is apparent in the intellectual resources drawn upon in framing the new "experiment of an extended republic."

> Is it not the glory of the people of America that, whilst they have paid a decent regard to the opinion of former times . . . they have not suffered a blind veneration for antiquity . . . to overrule the suggestions of their own good sense. . . . To this manly spirit posterity will be indebted for the possession . . . of numerous innovations . . . in favor of private rights and public happiness.[57]

In addition, this outlook is apparent in the very fact of writing "from scratch," a fundamental law which will, in turn, provide the contours for subsequent, lesser laws and policies, and which, while it can itself be altered, can be done so only with difficulty, and even then in a process which cannot legally alter its fundamental character.

> If such a revolution should ever happen from causes which the foresight of man cannot guard against, the House of Representatives with the people on their side, will at all times be able *to bring back the Constitution to its primitive form and principles.*[58] (Emphasis added.)

A second characteristic of the *Federalist*'s constitution, which will serve to set it off from democracy, is the idea that it is a compounded or mixed republic whose stability resides in the equilibrium between opposing forces—between dependence and independence, order and liberty, energy and stability, ambition and ambition, duty and interest, branches of government, the militia and the regular army, principles of proportional and equal representation, commerce and agriculture, different commercial interests, religious denominations, and so on.[59] By inference, if this approach to reconciling oppositions without eliminating them is institutionalized in a fundamental law, it should also, over time, be apparent in the characters of those citizens nurtured under it.

A third important characteristic of the *Federalist*'s constitution (for our analysis) is the object of its endeavors. Its highest public aim appears to be freedom or formal equality, based on deference toward diversity of individual talents and pursuits:

> spirit which activates the people of America . . . a spirit which nourishes freedom, and in return is nourished by it.[60]

> The diversity in the faculties of men, from which the rights of property originate. . . . The protection of these faculties is the first object of government.[61]

A final characteristic of the *Federalist*'s republicanism which I note for later reference, is its approach to the use of military force. Publius observes that "safety from external danger is the most powerful director of national conduct," and that means and resources allotted to the military "ought to be proportional to the end" of providing for the common defense.[62] On the other hand, America is also referred to as a "flourishing empire." It appears that Publius has here modified Machiavelli's claim in the *Discourses on Livy*, that republics which rely upon the people for the preservation of liberty must be expansionist as was Rome, by implying that expansion can be largely commercial, and, hence, apparently not aggressive.

Summary

Drawing upon the insights of the various theorists and writers examined thus far, I believe we can retain our initial identification of the republican as one who resists specialization in the personality to the point or degree at which it no longer feels some responsibility for the preservation of its governmental authority, understood as the context for political action (as well as private pursuits) among formal equals. Such a specification of character implies that one is capable of grasping intellectually, the distinction between a general set of arrangements for the general good, and what occurs within them; and capable morally and psychologically of living with the tensions which will necessarily arise between the public and private in such a complex and independent orientation. By implication, such a character must be capable of practical action to preserve the general arrangements or institutions of authority within which more specialized aims are pursued; this will entail, as well, the prudent judgment to know when and where to assert one's private rights and claims, and when to refrain from doing so. As the foregoing illustrates, such characters are clearly presumed in the pages of the *Federalist*. Let us move on to examine their subsequent fortunes as seen in subsequent reflections on the evolution of the American polity.

de Tocqueville

De Tocqueville's *Democracy in America* characterizes the American citizen of the 1830s as simply democratic, and observes that this character operates on the principle of "self-interest rightly understood."[63] The question for our analysis is whether de Tocqueville's democrat (distinguished only from the aristocrat) any longer fits the description of republican character, and if so, where. Here it is perhaps useful to remind ourselves summarily of the characteristics of this character, in order to facilitate comparison with de Tocqueville's "democrat." We have tentatively identified the republican as one who resists specialization of the personality to a point or degree at which it no longer feels some responsibility for the preservation of the *authority* of its government, understood as the context for genuine political action among relative equals.

In the case of modern "mass" politics, this responsibility may come down most of the time to following issues of public concern and discussing them with others; selecting candidates for office in terms broader and more distant than immediate self-interest solely; serving in the military and on juries and local committees when called upon to do so; and paying taxes and making charitable and campaign donations. But the kernel of this character is still, adjusted for historical circumstances, the ideal of balance between extreme dependence and extreme independence. And it can manifest itself either in a more "Greek" way as the capacity to view and feel responsibility for the political and social system as a whole; or in a more "Roman" way as the capacity to see and act upon the singular importance for political life of authoritative procedures and laws as the basis for civic obligation.[64] How, then, does de Tocqueville's "democrat" appear in this light?

Before answering, it is useful to recall de Tocqueville's general thesis in *Democracy in America:* that the tendency of unchecked democracy is toward a centralized government providing equal and material benefits to an increasingly dependent and homogeneous population submerged in the gratification of "suburban" pleasures at the expense of public duties.[65] And, the American of the 1830s, he observed, resisted this unpolitical, materialist tendency through institutions of local governance requiring his participation, and through the influence of (nonmaterialist) religion directing his energies to more transcendent objects.[66] De Tocqueville also noted that the Americans were fond of combating tendencies of private selfishness through "the principle of self-interest rightly understood," which led them to identify some public sacrifice as a form of their own self-interest. Still, de Tocqueville was not especially sanguine that this outlook could be relied upon over time to keep free the public realm, and spoke explicitly of the need for giving to a democratic people "the rights and the political character which may impart to every citizen some of those interests that cause the nobles to act for the public welfare in aristocratic countries."[67]

De Tocqueville's general teaching, then, appears to be that a healthy democracy will be one which takes from aristocracy the love of local and individual freedom, and the habits and institutions necessary to preserve it ("nothing but the love and habit of freedom can maintain an advantageous contest with the love and habit of physical well-being.")[68] The answer to our question, then, would seem to be that the democratic character which still has responsibility for the details of local governance, and which still has some transcendent or religious impulses in it, resembles at least our account of the republican character.

Still, it should be noted as we proceed, that the emphasis of de Tocqueville's account is never upon the common good or public duty, per se, and rests for its cogency and effect upon self-interest being understood in expansive and "enlightened" terms. Unlike eighteenth-century writers such as Hamilton and Kant, de Tocqueville no longer juxtaposes duty and interest, or duty and happiness, but attempts to explain the former as a version of the latter. And, unlike Aristotle and Machiavelli, de Tocqueville (perhaps in reaction to Napoleonic excesses) did not think that a "manly love of order" is learned in military service (for the majority of people) and transferred to civil life, but apparently the reverse.

James Fenimore Cooper

Although not a political theorist, James Fenimore Cooper makes some observations interesting from the standpoint of our distinction between the republican and democratic characters. These are to be explicitly found in Cooper's nonfiction work, *The American Democrat,* written in 1838. Observing changes in America upon return from an extended stay in Europe, Cooper was interested in distinctions within democracy which the aristocrat de Tocqueville did not observe. "De Tocqueville could not take seriously the limited social stratification which persisted within a radical equality of conditions."[69]

Although Cooper does not explicitly distinguish between *republic* and *democracy* (and, in fact, uses the terms interchangeably), he is interested in the differences between better and worse democracies, and is clearly concerned about the loss of independence, individuality, and solid character occurring in America with the growth of the powers of the press, organized political parties, and urban commercial centers such as New York City. These forces were turning America away from true democracy, in his view, toward rule by fluctuating public opinion manipulated by "political agents."[70] In other words, true or good democracy for Cooper is what I am calling a republic or regime built upon middling standards of decency, deference, and formal equality in the midst of genuine social diversity. Cooper, in spite of an elitist reputation as the son of a Federalist, was so hostile to aristocracy (which he equated with oligarchy) that he could not take seriously the claim of aristocrats such as Plato and de Tocqueville, that ever-expanding rule by increasingly egalitarian public opinion, was the natural tendency of democracy—he simply viewed this as a danger to be avoided.

Two things in particular concerned Cooper about the evolutions he observed in the American republic (sometimes American democracy). One was the loss of independent judgment arising in deference to "public opinion," rather than to what was really true, which Cooper never doubts can be determined even in political matters. (The doctrinaire democrat, Steadfast Dodge, in Cooper's novel, *Homeward Bound*, is always striving to create "a public opinion," and even desires to form a committee to judge the accuracy of the ship captain's navigation.[71]) Cooper's other major concern was the public deference he observed in the years following the presidency of Andrew Jackson, by political leaders to the values of the "common man." All of this led, in Cooper's view, to the displacement of the will of the whole people as reflected in the Constitution and in legal institutions, by the will of a part (majority) of the people at any given moment, and hence to a subversion of the republic.[72] (On this point, Cooper is reminiscent of Rousseau's arguments in the *Social Contract*, although he never uses the latter's terminology.)

The developments which Cooper was describing in the 1830s and 1840s do not really receive a philosophical defense, and find rhetorical and legal expression at the highest levels, until the presidency of Woodrow Wilson (and later FDR). These subsequent developments in the American system also highlight the importance of having a distinction in usage between republic and democracy (or having a name for a form of popular government which still retains formalistic aspects alien to the democratic *ethos*), as Aristotle and the *Federalist* authors have, and Plato, de Tocqueville, and Cooper do not.

Woodrow Wilson

If de Tocqueville stretched democratic presuppositions as far as they could go in approximating the republican outlook, the rhetoric and political program of Pres. (and political scientist) Woodrow Wilson unambiguously gave up that project. This can be seen by contrasting Wilson's outlook with that of the *Federalist.*

The intent of the writers and defenders of the Constitution of 1787, especially as evidenced in the essays of Madison, was to maintain a realm of public freedom through devices of institutional equilibrium which would make it impossible for any department, state, or individual to aggrandize power sufficient to close down the realm of freedom for others. The writers of the *Federalist* place their reliance on the mechanics of the Constitution; the ability of at least some of the citizens of the United States to grasp and appreciate these arrangements;[73] and the size and diversity of America, to produce outcomes friendly to the country as a whole, rather than to sectional or party interest.

What qualifies this outlook as "republican," is the overriding concern that considerations of private and substantive interest be continuously weighed against the duty to preserve the general system of institutional equilibrium making pursuit of private interests—economic, religious, familial, and so on—possible for a wide variety and diversity of citizens. In this respect, the general orientation of the *Federalist* is reminiscent of the outlook of Trenchard and Gordon in *Cato's Letters* a half-century earlier:

> And though in pursuing Views, Men regard themselves and their own Advantages; yet if they regard the Publick more, or their own in Subservience to the Publick, they may justly be esteemed virtuous and good.[74]

Now, this tension between these two concerns is clearly absent in the outlook of the American president explicitly concerned not merely to foster a democratic *ethos,* but to "democratize" the Constitution—Woodrow Wilson.[75]

> We are the first Americans to hear our own countrymen ask whether the Constitution is still adapted to serve the purposes for which it was intended . . . the first to think of remodeling the administrative machinery of the federal government, and of forcing new forms of responsibility upon Congress. . . . The noble charter of 1787 . . . is now our *form of government* rather in name than in reality. . . .[76]

To appreciate this change in general outlook, let us begin by putting Wilson's aims in historical context. Like the legislators of the antebellum South, Wilson was convinced that the Madisonian system of constitutional equilibrium had broken down through the concentration of economic power. In this case, large corporations had gained, in addition to concentrated economic power, control of state legislatures and thus of the national senate as well. In Wilson's view, radical reform of the government was necessary to preserve meaningful freedom for the majority of citizens, whose inherent conservatism and deference were allowing them to be led by leaders they had never chosen. Of interest for our analysis is Wilson's approach to gaining support for his vision of reform (and even secular redemption).[77]

Over a period of several decades in both academic and popular writing and speech, Wilson began to make the argument that we did not have to be bound by the Constitution, and certainly did not have to show deference to it. Wilson was fond of saying that *nothing* in the country was the same as even twenty years before; that we were continually evolving, and that Darwin not Newton should be our constitutional analogue.

> The trouble with the (Federalist) theory is that government is not a machine, but a living thing. . . . It is accountable to Darwin, not to Newton. . . . *No living thing can have its organs offset against each other, as checks, and live. . . .*[78] (Emphasis added.)

And where were we evolving? Toward an age of the "common man" for whom enlightened leaders and neutral administrators would help to provide.

> Nobody who cannot speak the common thought, who does not move by the common impulse, is the man to speak for America, or for any of her future purposes.[79]

> Therefore, we have got to organize a government . . . which will consult as large a proportion of the people of the United States as possible before its acts. Because the great problem of government is to know what the average man is experiencing and thinking about.[80]

The general point for our analysis is that nowhere in the political rhetoric and outlook of Wilson (and later FDR) does one see even the intimation of the idea of preserving a system of public authority in which substantive interests would also have political meaning. Rather, in Aristotelian terms, the economic program of the "oligarchs" is simply to be replaced by that of the "democrats" (as formulated by *illuminati*); and, if there is an implication of the common good, it is to be identified with the good of the democrat, understood as efficient "social progress" or the betterment of the living conditions of greater numbers of people. The price, it seems, for containing the power of an economic oligarchy who grew to maturity in an age of expansion and production, was their replacement by enlightened leaders at least chosen by the "common man" to look after his interests.

What we can see, then, in the achievements of Woodrow Wilson and the progressive movement is the public endorsement and codification of the incipient changes in customs and manners (away from independent judgment) described by Cooper in 1838: the citizen of the U.S. democratic system is no longer to attempt to preserve the internal tension which arises in weighing his needs against those of the public authority and the common good. Rather, he is simply to specialize in looking after his own needs, and those of his family, and to place his trust in leaders who understand these needs and will formulate them for him. This democratic version of a citizen who is to turn concern for broad questions of context over to his leaders, is nowhere more apparent than in Wilson's influential essay on the study of public administration.

> The bulk of mankind is rigidly unphilosophical, and nowadays the bulk of mankind's votes. . . .[81]

> The problem is to make public opinion efficient, without suffering it to be meddlesome.[82]

This change in the ideal of a citizen toward a kind of one-sided simplicity can be further illustrated by reference to FDR's famous "Commonwealth Club" speech, delivered during the presidential campaign of 1932, and "often cited as Roosevelt's clearest expression of his general economic and political views." In this speech, Roosevelt, "glad for this opportunity to discuss with you what it all means to me," argues that because "we are steering a steady course toward economic oligarchy," real leadership of America must pass to "enlightened administration," which will adapt "existing economic organizations to the service of the people." This is consistent with the requirements of democracy, which is nothing but "a quest, a never-ending seeking for better things"; and with the requirements of the statesman, whose "greatest duty" is "to educate," and to provide for the definition of the people's rights. Our direction must be toward "a permanently safe order of things," and an economic declaration of rights which guarantees "the right to make a comfortable living."[83]

The picture which emerges by implication is that politics is really about a power struggle *between* the democratic masses led by enlightened leaders, and an entrenched oligarchy, in which struggle the people either serve the government or are served by it. Clearly absent in FDR's political vision is the idea of a middling standard in which citizens both serve and are served by government because they are responsible both for and to it, that is, see themselves as at least partly political, rather than simply as providers for the needs of themselves and their families (through alliances with powerful patrons, in or out of government).

Restatement of the Problem

We have now covered enough ground to make a more systematic attempt at a distinction between the republican and democratic characters, which can span the political experience of over two millennia, and hopefully still be meaningful. To phrase this differently, is there a way to characterize Aristotle's distinction between the highest form of democracy (a regime of laws favorable to the "many") and the lowest form of polity (a regime of laws favorable to the "common advantage"), which will allow us to apply it outside of ancient Greek historical experience? Or, a way to characterize Machiavelli's observations on the Roman republic which is meaningful outside of Renaissance Italy, and so on? The common element in all our discusions of a republic has to do with the recognition by citizens, of the importance of a common good, or a realm of public authority as the context for other pursuits,[84] and a meaningful way of explaining this characteristic across time is in terms of understanding time at any particular time.[85]

Republics and Time

The view I have to present is that regardless of the particular language used in the historical circumstances, one important distinction between the republican and the democratic character, is a different and more expansive sense of *time*, which makes meaningful and real, the problem of a general good, and of achievement and preservation of public authority. For whatever complex, evolutionary reasons, the personality usually called "democratic" is incapable of grasping the problem of the general good as real—it largely remains for this personality "epiphenomenal," or, even fraudulent. Perhaps this is why Aristotle found that the distinguishing excellence of the polity was the use of arms[86]— that is to say by implication, that military service is a concrete way of grasping and acting upon the issue of the common good (or a common object of good) for the majority of people.

To pursue this line of reasoning, what I designate the republican character has a more complex time-sense than the democratic, and possibly than the aristocratic, as well. It is a time-sense constituted in a *tension between* the more transient and appetitive aspects of experience, *and* the more enduring and general aspects, *both of which* are grasped as important and real. The various debates over civic corruption since the Renaissance, and the various ways to combat it—military service, agrarian occupations, and enlightened self-interest—are illuminated by viewing the problem in this light; in addition, I believe it makes Aristotle's distinction between the highest form of democracy (still a partisan regime), and the lowest form of republic (mixed government) clearer for us.

Let me try to restate the problem starting with the issue of civic corruption and its relation to time-sense. The common element I see in almost all historic debates over civic corruption is the idea of extreme dependency, whether upon a dictator, or upon powerful economic interests, or upon personal appetite, *or upon one another*. Power, in such situations, becomes increasingly "phenomenal," immediate, and unstable, as it is based more on perceptions about what others are likely to do, rather than upon fixed or more abiding forms of influence such as constitutional authority, physical prowess, or shock of arms. As more power calculations focus (through growth and ease of communication) upon the likely and contingent effect of every word and action of the circumstantially powerful—the dictator, the masses, the market—the predominant sense of time becomes "phenomenal" rather than seasonal, cyclical, or even transcendent. To say this in more conventional language, in extremely democratic situations, where every shift in power perceptions is of "constitutional" significance, there is soon no constitution (or ordering) in actual fact. On the other hand, a time-sense which is so disdainful of the contingent, the phenomenal, and the appetitive as to exclude them from constitutional significance, in its political form would be called "true aristocracy" (total dedication to the public good), and in its philosophical form, "Platonic" (true reality as a realm of pure ideas.)[87] What I am calling the "republican character," spans these two time-senses by incorporating them as a tension in a single citizen, under a constitutional system making such an outlook viable. I believe this was the outlook of the most intelligent and influential among the founders of the United States, and is also the basis for the stability of their system. That is to say, the stability resides in the comprehensiveness of the outlook nurtured by their constitutional arrangements, incorporating (for different seasons) three human ways of viewing time—as the never changing (e.g., maxims about human nature and ambition), the slowly changing (e.g., customs and laws), and the ever changing (e.g., policies and the market).

Such a view of the republican character, as one grounded in an uneasy tension between the immediate and the recurring (or abiding), may assist us in finding a common ground in various historical ideals which we have inherited as "republican." Consider in this regard the following claims—that the republican character is not atheistic;[88] that it bears some relation to the country and agriculture; that it can be constituted in "enlightened" commerce as well; that it is capable of competently bearing arms; that it is "amateurish" (i.e., resists extreme specialization in the personality); that it cares for the common or general good, or is habituated to "civic virtue"; that it has its origins in the traditional family, and so on.

Each of these emphases has the effect of resisting extreme dependence on forms of power and influence generated exclusively by perceptions and calculations about likely shifts in power—that is, they all anchor the personality in something outside of the ephemeral, while permitting it, in varying degrees, to value as well the transient, the contingent, or the appetitive event. For example, belief in dependence on a Creator; dependence on the soil; belief in the utility of the abstraction of "self-interest rightly understood"; and the abstract capacity to grasp the importance of a public realm of action and meaning, all move the personality away from radical dependence on the short-term perceptions of others, and toward generation of a tension within the individual between dependence and independence, characteristic of, for example, Aristotle's middling citizen. Military service (and gentlemanly "amateurishness" generally)[89] moves the personality toward a tension between thought and action, and between authority and appetite (as in the case of the soldier prepared one minute to use lethal force to disarm a member of an opposing military force, and the next to care for him as a dependent once he is disarmed and helpless). In the same vein, the deference learned toward the authority of parents in traditional families, while strictly speaking a more monarchical than republican characteristic, may provide an initial understanding of formal authority (distinguished from mere power) for those born in otherwise democratic regimes.

Thus, I am led to the view that a meaningful account of the republican character can be given which spans both ancient and modern experience, and which distinguishes it from the true aristocrat's complete devotion to the common good, on the one hand, and from the democratic preoccupation with appetitive self-interest, on the other. It turns out to be a character characterized by a middle position, existing in the tension between the ephemeral and the recurring; appetite and authority; and between dependence and independence with regard to others. If there is a significant distinction between ancient and modern forms of this republican belance, it might be in the tendency of the ancient Greco-Roman world to locate the balance (in the regime as a whole) between classes, and in the modern world to locate the balance self-consciously in individual citizens. But for our purposes in analyzing political character, too much is not to be made of this difference. Ancient writers such as Aristotle and Cicero strained toward the equivalent of the modern ideal, and modern defenders of commerce such as Adam Ferguson harkened back to ancient ideals of wholeness. For example, Aristotle's polity is grounded in the middle-class individual who understands the claims of both the oligarch and the democrat; Cicero made it a major theme of his essay on duties *(De Officiis)* that the state exists to protect private property; and Ferguson wrote in his essay on the history of civil society (1767), that to continue the otherwise healthy specialization of the arts and professions into the realm "of the arms which form the citizen . . . the arts of policy and war, is an attempt to dismember the human character. . . ."[90]

By different routes then, I am led back to the view that there is a distinctive republican character discernible *here and there* across two and a half millennia of Western political reflection, distinguished by the complexity of its allegiances to things both private and public. I have tried to view it as constituted in a complex time-sense capable of maintaining a healthy tension among the poles or dimensions of various intersecting axes[91]—

the recurring and the ephemeral, duty and appetite, and thought[92] and action. I have suggested that the hallmark of this character is the ability to *grasp* the significance of a realm of public authority, and without being single-mindedly devoted to it, still sacrifice for its preservation. Finally, I have suggested that an important issue for us—in an age of increasing specialization of personalities and professions—is to distinguish the republican character from its less complex (or less mixed) and more highly specialized sibling, "the democrat."

The character I am describing can be either partisan in the Burkean sense ("When bad men combine, good men must associate"), or staunchly unpartisan, or sufficiently versatile as to be capable of following Machiavelli's advice to play both the fox and the lion—it depends for our purposes on the larger intention. So long as the intent is to achieve some substantive interest for oneself or one's supporters, while still preserving a public realm of freedom under general laws, sustained by competition in government and party, I believe we have evidence of the republican character—such as, Adlai Stevenson, who while running for president of the United States as a member of the Democratic party, is reported to have felt that the Republicans should win if we were to have a much-needed, nonpartisan foreign policy.[93] (A personality concerned *solely* with the preservation of this realm would begin to qualify as "statesmanlike" in the Aristotelian sense.) By contrast, the democratic character sees those in government as simply other competitors for resources and influence; or if himself already in government or military service, sees his function as the aggrandizement of resources and influence for himself and his supporters, as an end in itself.[94] Yet, anytime we find individuals raised within a commercial democratic *ethos* of material self-interest and individual happiness, who can still grasp[95] the idea of political authority as providing the context for this pursuit (rather than as simply another form of it), we are on the trail of our catch. The democratic character is generally incapable of recognizing the difference in actual practice *between* the authoritative context for substantive transactions, *and* the transactions themselves, perhaps because such a "context" has sufficient permanence and abstraction (generality) as to move it outside of the ephemeral, democratic time-sense. To say this more historically, the democratic character will generally have a very incomplete view of how much of his present circumstances is owed to his politically minded forbears. Let me try to illustrate in more concrete terms.

Texas, Petitioner v. Gregory Lee Johnson

An unambiguous illustration of the outlook of the democratic character can be found in a passage of the legal reasoning of Supreme Court Justice William Brennan in the recent "flag-burning" case. One of the issues treated was whether public burning and denunciation of the flag fell within "the 'small class of fighting words' that are likely to provoke the average person to retaliation, and thereby cause a breach of peace." Brennan's reasoning on this point is remarkable from the standpoint of our analysis of the differences between the republican and democratic characters. In what appears to be an unguarded and candid statement, Brennan is extremely revealing about the outlook of the democratic character. "No reasonable onlookers would have regarded Johnson's generalized expression of dissatisfaction with the policies of the Federal Government as a direct personal insult, *or as an invitation to exchange fisticuffs.*"[96] (Emphasis added.)

The revealing implication is that in Brennan's mind, no "reasonable onlooker" could be driven to physical violence over a political abstraction or symbol, accompanied by the words, *"America . . . we spit on you."*[97] Now, as an empirical matter, this is simply wrong—any number of "reasonable onlookers," who at an impressionable age had served in the military and had sworn an oath to protect and defend the Constitution against all enemies, foreign and domestic, might have regarded Johnson's actions as "an invitation to exchange fisticuffs." But Brennan's unguarded statement is more interesting as a revelation of the assumptions of the unpolitical, democratic personality—that it is not "reasonable" to fight over political abstractions (and their symbolic equivalents) such as duty, honor, and the common good,[98] because, by implication, these are not *real*. And how different is Brennan's viewpoint from that of the Court in 1907.

> Hence, it has often occurred that insults to the flag have been the cause of war, and indignation put upon it, in the presence of those who revere it, have often been resented and sometimes punished upon the spot.[99]

Yet, it is in the dissenting opinion of Justice John Paul Stevens that we can observe the kinds of distinctions associated with the republican character, distinctions boh elusive and obscure (because not "real") for the democratic personality. Stevens argues (sounding very much like Aristotle on the meaning of a regime or constitution) that the flag is more than a symbol of national unity; it is a symbol of the ideas which characterize our society, in this case liberty and equality. Hence the flag as a symbol is a unique case. "The question is unique. In my judgment rules that apply to a host of other symbolism such as state flags, armbands . . . are not necessarily controlling." He then goes on to suggest that the Court was "quite wrong" in asserting that the respondent "was prosecuted for his expression of dissatisfaction with the policies of the country. . . ." Rather, on Stevens's view, there is a qualitative difference between "policies" and fundamental ideas ("liberty" and "equality") which provide the context within which specific policies are pursued; and hence the "trivial burden" placed upon free expression by channeling dissatisfaction with policies into other modes does not outweigh the damage done in desecration of the unique symbol of our fundamental ideas as a society.[100]

For our analysis, there are then two important, logically implied differences in the reasoning of Justices Stevens and Brennan. Stevens makes a *qualitative* distinction between fundamental ideas (the authoritative context for policies), and particular policies, and Brennan does not, by implication treating them all as "homogeneous" in his interpretation of Johnson's actions and words as expressions of "dissatisfaction with the policies of the country." Secondly, Stevens treats political abstractions such as "liberty" and "equality" as real and motivating on their own, while Brennan, by implication, does not, in arguing that no "reasonable onlooker" could have taken Johnson's desecration of the flag and chant *("Red, white, and blue, we spit on you")* as "fighting words." (Apparently, for Brennan, "fighting words" could only mean a personal insult.[101]) And these differences highlight the blindness of the advanced, democratic personality: in its fixation with short-term, individual and collective physical, material and (lower) psychic well-being,[102] it forgoes the ability to grasp the *full* meaning of higher-order political abstractions, such as the "common good," or "political authority," controlling ideas with important practical effects which lose their force when reduced to mere rationalizations for someone's (or some group's) substantive program and interests.

Republicanism and Liberalism

What is the relationship of our distinction between the republican and democratic characters to the various articulations of civil and political life characteristic of the Liberalism of the past two centuries? I believe it is important to indicate a general answer to this question, by way of showing the relevance of this inquiry for modern politics and political theory.

At first, it might seem that Liberal theories of state and civil society, placing individual conscience, rights, and privacy before political authority in importance, would be at odds with the kind of public orientation necessary for the appelation, "republican." But, this need not be the case. The important issue here, as I see it, is whether the theory or theorist in question has for a goal or focus, the idea of citizens who are caretakers of a public way of life (their particular version of civility), as well as agents of their own private interests; citizens who are capable in their public personae of treating as real, and *acting upon*, something as general and abstract as the idea of "the rule of law," or "our way of life," or "civilized behavior." Thus, theorists within the (generally) Liberal tradition of the past few centuries who have emphasized forms of authority, individual judgment, and *general* arrangements would better fit our description of republican, than those Liberal writers who have stood upon rights to certain material benefits or social goods, as the focus of political or social justice.

The major issue, again, for the purpose of specifying "republicanlike" within the Liberal tradition, is whether citizens are seen as carying within themselves a conceptual grasp of the broader (and more enduring) political context for the realization of their particular interests, as well as the will to nourish and preserve that broader context as reflected in institutions, practices, laws, and so on. On this view, the writings of the twentieth-century philosopher of individualism, Michael Oakeshott, with their view of civil association as having neither extrinsic nor substantive purpose,[103] shows affinities with republicanism, in spite of Oakeshott's "theoretical" aversion to politics and things military. Other modern theorists, emphasizing "participation" and activism as the means to procure certain material goods (or simply as an economic pressure release), do not show these affinities with the republican character. This point can be made clearer by contrasting Oakeshott's "classical liberalism" with that of the "welfare liberalism" of the theorist John Rawls.

However, before turning to either Oakeshott or Rawls, some consideration is in order of John Locke, the seventeenth-century English theorist of limited government and individual rights, later influential in prerevolutionary America and afterward.[104] The interesting question for our analysis is whether the Lockean "gentleman" (whose education and political and religious principles Locke set forth in *Some Thoughts Concerning Education, Two Treatises of Government,* and several religious tracts), is closer to our republican or democratic character.

Locke

The basic Lockean viewpoint is well-known and may be briefly summarized. Government comes into being through rational consent of the governed for the sake of the "publick good," understood primarily as the protection of property, where property, in turn, is understood expansively to mean natural rights to "life, liberty and estate."[105] The natural right to property is derivative of a duty to God and others to preserve ourselves and a general way of life in which we can live "rationally." As Locke says of this duty, "The taking away of God, even in thought only, dissolves all."[106] Though Locke wished to remove religious and pedagogical orientation (characterized by moderate self-reliance) as inculcated by families and tutors especially from the purview of government coercion, this was the anchor for the restraint and trust necessary for the maintenance of the Lockean political and economic "system." Duties toward others then, while not properly a political matter in the Lockean lexicon, were assumed through consciousness of the relationship of each individual to a common creator,[107] and through a "rational" conception of civility taught by families and set forth in Locke's treatise on education.

The essence of this education has been summarized concisely by Nathan Tarcov.

> Separate though it may be, the gentleman's education Locke advocates is supportive of the politics he taught. It forms men of business

> and affairs. They are physically fit and courageous, able to be soldiers if necessary . . . they are willing and able to concern themselves with their estates, perhaps even with trade, and to be active and informed in public affairs. To this end, they know their country's history and laws . . . they are . . . free men, independent and self-reliant. (but) They are sensitive to praise and blame, to the power of public opinion. They are well-informed to further the public interest by attending to private property while being at the same time vigilant observers of government. . . .[108]

Now, this description is not far from our description of the republican character, with the exception that the emphasis here is on attending to public business solely for protection of a private space in which to raise families, worship, and acquire and improve property, rather than on maintaining a tension between public and private in the individual citizen for the sake of balance itself. The description is certainly *not* very similar to our specialized "democrat."

However, one salient problem with these Lockean characters and their civil and political arrangements, is that they have no internal, long-range resistance to the corruption of civic duty if belief in God as the basis of common duties wanes, since they make no provision for a public education system to preserve these central religious beliefs, and, in fact, are set up formally to separate politics and religion. Hence the emphasis on acquisition and improvement of property as a form of religious praise[109] is especially subject to vulgarization and excess, if atheism and immanentist philosophy flourish[110] at the expense of forms of transcendence—a situation which de Tocqueville explicitly warned American democracy to avoid. Thus, the short (and somewhat schematic) answer to our question, would appear to be that the Lockean gentleman, less the transcendent basis for his duties to others (military training forming no central part of his character), mutates slowly and steadily into the "democratic" character standing on his "natural" rights to acquisition solely for its own sake.

Michael Oakeshott

Although it begins from largely individualist and nominalist presuppositions, Michael Oakeshott's theoretical account of civil association, and his critique of modern Rationalism, do show certain affinities with what I have identified as the republican tradition and character (rather than the democratic[111]). For our purposes in distinguishing between the two characters, it is interesting to identify three. The first is Oakeshott's starting point, which is not the priority of rights, or of rights over duties, but an account of the nature of obligation to authority. In a democratic age, hostile to abstraction, and inclined to identify the vocabulary of politics and governance with an enterprise about the concentration of power to distribute substantive benefits to various groups, and attribute legitimacy to those who can deliver the "goods," Oakeshott tries to discipline our attention sufficiently long to derive or rejuvenate an entire civil vocabulary from an initial idea of being associated in terms of a "practice of civility," or in terms of the recognition of "rules as rules." He distinguishes between association to accomplish some substantive purpose (e.g., feeding the poor or saving souls), and association in terms of rules too general to specify concrete, substantive purposes, and hence capable of serving as the terms of association themselves.[112] On Oakeshott's account, a citizen is one capable of grasping and assenting to a general authoritative context, while pursuing private purposes within the world they make possible.

> The only understanding of *respublica* capable of evoking the acceptance of all *cives* without exception, and thus eligible to be recognized as the terms of association, is *respublica* understood in terms of its authority.[113]

> *Respublica*, a practice of civility specifying . . . conditions to be subscribed to in choosing performances, and therefore the common or "public" concern, not the common purposes of *cives*.[114]

A first affinity, then, between Oakeshott's *civis* and our republican character is the willingness (not merely to live with, but) to nourish the tension between particular goals and concern for the general framework of authority ("the public concern") within which they are achieved. To say this differently, both are characterized by a generalist (even "amateurish") orientation resistant to extreme specialization of energy or attention directed exclusively toward success in substantive enterprises.

A second affinity with the republican tradition in Oakeshott's account of civil association is the room it leaves for deference among genuinely diverse characters for one another's respective talents. Oakeshott is especially concerned about giving a theoretical articulation of the historic European *ethos* (since the breakup of the medieval realms) to be distinct, to cultivate the freedom to choose inherent in moral agency. But this attitude or habit of distinctness and self-reliance can be at home in a situation of what has been called "republican deference," in a way that it cannot be at home within the democratic *ethos* of equality of conditions described by de Tocqueville in *Democracy in America* ("But for equality their passion is ardent, insatiable, incessant, invincible."[115]). As J.G.A. Pocock has observed, "deference was not a hierarchical but a republican characteristic," arising in the respect different kinds of people held for different kinds of virtues and talents, and permitting the individual to know himself "through the respect shown by his fellows for the qualities publicly recognized in him."[116] And this was distinguished from the democratic developments toward conformity and uniformity de Tocqueville was beginning to observe in Jacksonian America (and to the dismay of Cooper).

> But once men were, or it was held they ought to be all alike, his only means of self-discovery lay in conforming to everybody's notions of what he ought to be and was. This produced a despotism of opinion since nothing but diffused general opinion now defined the ego or its standard of judgment.[117]

Pocock's point (and Harrington and Cooper's before him) is that genuine deference comes from the individual and is at home neither in aristocracy-oligarchy where hierarchy is institutionalized, nor in democracy where all are presumed to have the same basic wants and needs; it can only properly exist in a republic or a civil association which cultivates a public *ethos* of formal equality but not sameness of substantive wants. We might also observe in passing, that this *ethos* to be self-reliant and distinct, characteristic of both modern republicanism and Oakeshott's classical liberalism, also leads away from the extreme civic and psychic dependence upon one another and *upon strong leaders*, censured by republican critics of democracy from Thucydides to opponents of the New Deal.

There is yet a third correspondence in Oakeshott's work with republicanism, and this resides in the general nature of his critique of modern Rationalism. "Rationalism" is Oakeshott's expression for what he calls *the* major European intellectual disposition of the past three centuries. He sees it as flowing from a vulgarization of some of the ideas of Bacon and Descartes, and characterized by a belief in the sovereignty of techniques, ideologies, and moral codes, abstracted from concrete activities and applied universally.[118]

Oakeshott's critique of modern Rationalism is that it is based upon a series of illusions (that is, that techniques and ideologies are neither self-contained nor universally applicable) which rupture genuine practical skill in every activity they invade, from politics to cookery. My point here is that Oakeshott's critique of Rationalism has distinct similarities with traditional republican critiques of advanced democracies, advanced monarchies, and old cities, that is, that they lose their balance and lucidity by falling into extreme dependence on public and urbane opinions and conventions, a process with no homeostatic qualities of self-correction. Said differently, they come to equate conventional opinion with all of reality, or reality outside the city's walls,[119] at the expense of the stability and balance which come from preserving the various tensions between the more permanent and the ephemeral, between general practices and particular policies, between the urban and rural, and so on. Oakeshott's critique of the Rationalist as mistaking a part for the whole in collapsing the tension between the formal and substantive, is similar in spirit and effect to this republican critique.

John Rawls

The preceding excursion into Oakeshott's thought was meant to show that there are similarities to republicanism in classical liberalism's *ethos* of the self-reliant generalist, which are not evident in twentieth-century "welfare" liberalism. The latter has much stronger affinities with the tendencies of advanced democracy. Turn now, in that context, to the ideas of John Rawls's *Theory of Justice*, which has been characterized as a theoretical defense of the liberal welfare state, and even as providing for "a new foundation for a radical egalitarian interpretation of liberal democracy."[120] Rawls's basic ideas (and their subsequent modifications) are now fairly well-known. He attempts to give a more or less reasoned account of a just society based on the idea of fairness, which turns out to mean, inter alia, that social and economic inequalities "must be to the greatest benefit of the least advantaged members of society,"[121] "where "society" is understood as a kind of absolute from which there is no escape. "In justice as fairness men agree to share one another's fate."[122]

The popularity of Rawls's ideas precludes the necessity of a lengthy discussion of them here. Let us simply look at the ones which are interesting from the standpoint of the distinction between the republican and democratic characters. First, it is clear that Rawls's picture of a just society is not one of formal equals deferring to one another's particular talents and characteristics, and united in mutual understanding of their obligations to a system of political authority. There is virtually no discussion of the problem of political authority and political order, beyond the implied assumption that a government which provided the basic social primary "goods" (rights and liberties, opportunities and powers, income and wealth, and "a sense of one's own worth"[123]) as a matter of individual rights, and which tolerated various "life-plans" consistent with those rights, would not need fear violent revolution.

Secondly, one is struck at (what sounds like a fulfillment of de Tocqueville's prophecies about dangerous democratic developments) the dependency of citizens under "justice as fairness." Their conceptions of their own self-worth depend heavily upon the esteem of others, who, will, in turn, it appears, withhold their respect where the other social primary goods are lacking in a person. Self-reliance, the strength to hold conflicting duties and desires in balanced tension, and individual independence and judgment (except in *calculating* the likely success of alternative "life-plans") do not appear prominent in Rawlsian personae.

A third democratic aspect of Rawls's theory of justice is the radically egalitarian impulse behind the idea ("the original position"[124]) that justice requires negating insofar as possible natural and genetic talents, physical attributes, and other characteristics such as beauty and grace. Combined with the idea that society is to be viewed as a great "resource pool" devoted to the material and psychic relief of all, but especially the least advantaged, the general picture which emerges is similar to the one criticized as extremely democratic by theorists from Plato to Adam Ferguson, de Tocqueville, and Nietzsche: demand for guarantees of equality and individual happiness leading to no higher purpose than the maintenance of group or species solidarity, and masked behind the cry for individual diversity over marginalia in the midst of a prevalent conformity. To say this differently, Rawls's account of a just society (in contrast to Oakeshott's account of the civil condition) does not provide for sufficient separation of issues of formal legitimacy from those of substantive benefits, to be considered republicanlike. On the contrary, Rawls's account of a just society looks very much like what Oakeshott calls a corporation-aggregate to guarantee benefits to needy subscribers, and in this sense, must be considered subpolitical, or simply uninterested in "abstractions" such as constitutional forms.

To summarize my general point in this discussion of Oakeshott and Rawls, I have tried to show that some of the differences between the republican and democratic characters can be seen in the differences between classical and modern welfare liberalism, especially in the formal and general orientation of the "older" liberalism, with its emphasis on authoritative institutions as the basis for the contingent pursuit of particular goals and policies, distinguished from the democratic and welfarist attempt to secure certain concrete outcomes at the expense of formal considerations. I have chosen Oakeshott as a philosophically stronger representative of the classical Liberal position than Locke, because, even though a twentieth-century writer, Oakeshott gives a most logically coherent and economical account of a way to reconcile the general outlook of Renaissance and Reformation individualism with the older requirements of political and civil obligation. His account may be described as having stronger affinities with republics than with democracies.

The Republican Character and the Armed Forces

With Aristotle and Machiavelli I recognize that the capacity for military service is an essential part of the republican character, but for reasons which I have never seen made fully explicit by ancient, Renaissance, or contemporary writers.[125] Hamilton's argument in *Federalist #23* is a good starting point for the view I wish to present. Hamilton argues commonsensically, that the military capacity (authority and resources) of the new republic should take its bearings from the requirements for the common defense against external attack and internal convulsion. "The *means* ought to be proportional to the *end*."[126] Now the ability to grasp the idea of the common defense of a system of territorially extended political authority, and to act upon it, is a good "litmus test" for identifying the republican character, and for the following reasons.

Firstly, the idea of the common defense of a political union is an abstraction (whether grasped conceptually in a definition or visually in a symbol, e.g., a flag), and, as such, requires some ability to think generally. Furthermore, the willingness to act upon this idea, at risk of life or at least hardship, suggests that the abstraction of the common defense is treated as *real*, not simply as an epiphenomenon, as in Justice Brennan's explicit view (discussed earlier) that the words *"Red, white and blue, we spit on you,"* could not be considered fighting words.

Secondly, the idea of defense, properly understood to include initiatives to preclude and ward off attack,[127] comprehends the ability to imagine a future, undesirable state of affairs to be prevented by a lesser, immediate sacrifice, and as such, bespeaks a fairly complex time-sense, capable of transcending the pull of present appetite.

Thirdly, the ability to apply armed force, even in a technological age, requires entrance into the world of not only practical but physical action (and danger), and, as such, pulls the personality away from specialization in words and thoughts only (whether philosophical or calculative), and toward the independence of character which come with the ability to defend one's own existence and that of one's dependents. In this sense, military service in a thoughtful person, or even a calculative person, begins to form a character instilled with a tension between thought and physical action. This is perhaps the truth in the insight that military service was one way of making citizens out of an otherwise self-interested bourgeoisie; it also bespeaks Aristotle's view that citizenship bridges the gap between the reflective and bestial sides of human nature.

Fourthly, for individuals raised in a democratic society, military life may be their only opportunity to see rules strictly enforced; to see the utility in a system of authority; and to have the opportunity to issue commands themselves. Said differently, military service may be the opportunity to learn, as Aristotle said, "to rule and be ruled," by one another.

Finally, the very need for defense, and the hardship and horror which often accompany it, militate against sanguine and millennialist views of simple linear progress in which the old political problems and tensions no longer recur.

All of these aspects of taking part in the common defense resist tendencies toward extreme democracy in the human character. The abstraction and sacrifice pull away from democracy's appetitive and materialist tendencies by providing firsthand experience of responsibility for a common good. The requirement to be adept in a world of physical danger pulls away from the tendency of especially commercial democracy to specialize the personality (can it any longer be called "character?") in a world of mental calculation. The habits and skills of collective and self-defense move the personality away from the extreme dependence of relying on specialists in force (that is, police and mercenaries), exclusively. (Blackstone's *Commentaries* still expect the citizen to provide for his own defense until the police arrive.[128]) Experience in ruling and being ruled give insight into the problems of those in political office at any moment, and, hence, insight as well into whether they are abusing their authority or not. Finally, the habit of sacrificing and risking for a possible future state of affairs (that is, successful defense of one's own), combined with the horrors often associated with military efforts, all work to inculcate a fairly complex time-sense, which (against the strictly democratic view) mixes hope for a better world with realistic expectations about the recurring tensions in the past and present ones.

There are those who might object that most individuals do not enter military service for the reasons I have enumerated, but rather enter from legal necessity, and once engaged, exert themselves and take risks solely for the preservation of themselves and immediate comrades-in-arms. To this objection I would raise two considerations. First, there are some individuals, especially officers, who would, upon reflection, concur with the reasons for, and effects of, military service which I have expounded.[129] (I would even venture to speculate that the largest single reservoir left in the United States of what I have called "the republican character," is to be found among those who were for some period military officers.) Secondly, I believe that there is no one who begins to develop habits associated with military service, whose character is not to some extent pulled in the direction of what is logically implied (and actually occasionally occurs) in the provision of the common defense of a political union.

Conclusion

What perspective can possibly link together in a meaningful way the ostensibly disparate observations of this essay, spanning over two millennia of Western political experience and reflection? I have suggested that it is the distinction between the republican and democratic characters—the former bespeaking a complex outlook grounded in a manageable tension between thought and action (including military service), and between the recurring and the transient, and mediated by acts of individual judgment; the latter characterized by a simpler time-sense and a more specialized outlook, obviating much need for political judgment beyond management of a corporate purpose to satisfy felt needs.

The strength of the republican character, as I understand it, is in the balance of (often) opposing forces, interests and desires; the strength of the democratic character in the capability efficiently to develop, mobilize, and exploit technology and resources for the satisfaction of felt needs, owing in part to the absence within it of a political and moral purpose sufficiently distant, general and fixed, as to limit the generation of such needs, or state authoritatively when they had been satisfied.

Hence, by inspection of the respective characters involved in popular government, I have been led to a view (similar to Aristotle's view) that a republic, anchored in the middling elements, living under general laws, and capable of participating in the common defense,[130] is *the* form of popular government capable of achieving political equilibrium over time,[131] by resisting the democratic reduction of constitutional arrangements to a process for the efficient satisfaction of bodily and (lower) psychic needs. This latter development is certainly a possible way of living together, but a much more specialized way; less free; populated by simpler and more specialized "individuals"; and probably less content, in spite of its constant pursuit of personal happiness within "the joyless quest for joy." It is also characterized by the various vulnerabilities attendant upon extreme specialization in any system or civilization, in particular, loss of the general political skills necessary for regeneration or refounding in the event of major disruption, and for the general guidance to lessen the likelihood of such political disruption in the first place. All of this suggests what even modern democrats know, that "more democracy is not always a good thing," and hence the need for retaining and nourishing the influence and insight of as many as possible of our republican generalists, a requirement which entails first of all the ability to recognize how they differ from the typical character of advanced, commercial democracy.

1989–92

Notes

1. On this, one could cite Plato and Aristotle in the ancient world, and de Tocqueville in the modern.

2. I am following Aristotle here by implication, since, as we shall see, he assigns the generic word for constitution *(politeia)* to the constitution which relies on "political" means, such as persuasion, to work for the common "advantage."

3. I believe that my claim about the specialization of advanced democracy is not at odds with Socrates famous characterization of democracy (*Republic* of Plato, Book 8) as the regime in which everyone does everything. These two tendencies are "flip sides of the same coin." (Consider the modern academic world in which we simultaneously have extreme specialization combined with great enthusiasm for interdisciplinary programs.) The leisure and lack of order which permit one person to specialize in great detail, also permit another to dabble in everything. Thus, in one sense at least, a specialist in philosophy such as Plato is a democratic phenomenon—philosophy certainly did not arise at Sparta or Rome.

4. See, in this connection, Appendix A of this book, "Two Views of Aristotle's *Politics*."

5. Aristotle's logic here (*Politics*, 5, 9) is that more democracy is a tendency of any democracy, and that it progresses in the following way: "The democrat starts by assuming that justice consists in equality; he proceeds to identify equality with the sovereignty of the will of the masses; he ends with the view that 'liberty and equality' consists of 'doing what one likes.' The result of such a view is that in these extreme democracies each man lives as he likes—or as Euripides says, 'For any end he chances to desire.'" Modern historians of antiquity such as Christian Meier, are critical of Aristotle's criticism of democracy (Meier is silent on Aristotle's criticism of oligarchy), and with "the grandiose pretensions of political theory" which dared to find fault with the practice of Athenian democracy, as being simply a more sophisticated version of the views of the "old oligarch," and hence, partisan. Cf. David McLintock, trans, *The Greek Discovery of Politics* (Cambridge, Mass.: Harvard University Press, 1990), 153. The aim of the present essay is to suggest that this is not the case by showing that the problem which Aristotle identifies is perennial with democracy. For this tendency in modern democracy, see de Tocqueville, *Democracy in America*, 2, 2, 2, any edition.

6. Aristotle does say, on the positive side, that the livelihood of farmers provides good physical training for warfare. *Politics*, 6, 4, any edition.

7. Ibid., 7, 9.

8. Ibid., 3, 7.

9. Ibid., 3, 9.

10. Ibid., 4, 13. ("Heavy arms" as the sine qua non of the city's defense against oligarchic horse cavalry.)

11. Ibid. (Emphasis added.) See, also, Martin Ostwald, *From Popular Sovereignty to the Sovereignty of Law* (Berkeley: University of California Press, 1986), 23. "We can conclude that Cleisthenic democracy was more of a scheme idéal d'une republique des hoplites, than a democracy in the later sense of the term. . . ."

12. Aristotle, *Politics*, 4, 8 and 11. See, also Leslie G. Rubin, "The Republic of Aristotle: Politics and the Best Regime" (Ph.D. diss., Boston College, University Microfilms International, 1985), Introduction, sect. B, The Political Virtues of Middle-Class Rule," 4–11.

13. I reach this conclusion from Aristotle's argument in the *Politics* (4, 4), that the military function (along with the judicial and deliberative functions)

is *of a similar order* to the mind rather than the body, and, hence, more political than functions to satisfy the realm of necessity. This viewpoint is also the source of Aristotle's criticism of (extreme) democracy—it politicizes the realm of necessity. But, as Marx well discerned, to politicize the realm of necessity is to render the vocabulary of politics either redundant (an economic management vocabulary will do), or exploitative (a smoke screen for the allocation of material benefits to some class). Part of Marx's strategy for revolution became the attempt to show that all higher-order abstractions were simply expressions of material relations; the rest was illusion or "false consciousness." This played well with Marx's followers, but also obscured intricate, historically evolved concepts representating the allocation of both tangibles and intangibles. See, on this, Michael Oakeshott, "On the Character of a Modern European State," in *On Human Conduct* (London: Oxford University Press, 1975).

14. Aristotle, *Nicomachean Ethics*, 8, 11 and 5, any edition.

15. Ibid, 8, 10 and 6.

16. Thucydides, *History of the Peloponnesian War*, 8, 97, any edition.

17. For a recent criticism (from a sociological point of view) of the ancient idea of the "middling citizen," as meaningless, see Josiah Ober, *Mass and Elite in Democratic Athens* (Princeton, N.J.: Princeton University Press, 1989), 30 n. 70. Ober's "sociological" analysis misses entirely the import of participation in the common defense, and the ability of the middling citizen to grasp the ideas of political rule and political ordering.

18. P. J. Rhodes, "The Five Thousand in the Athenian Revolutions of 411 B.C.," *The Journal of Helenic Studies* 92 (1972): 127.

19. Polybius, *The Histories*, 6, 3, 3, any edition.

20. Cicero, *De Officiis*, 1, 7, any edition.

21. Ibid., 3, 29.

22. Ibid., 3, 6.

23. Ibid., 2, 21–22.

24. Polybius, *The Histories*, 6, 56.

25. Donald Earl, *The Moral and Political Tradition of Rome* (Ithaca, N.Y.: Cornell University Press, 1967), 63–64. The phrase "rule of law" can be misleading since, as Aristotle notes (*Politics*, 4, 4), there are higher (but still perverted) forms of democracy which live by rule of laws rather than immediate majority decision. The issue is whether or not the constitutional laws are general and directed toward uniting all parts of the body politic, or whether they are simply instrumental to the advantage of a particular class or group. The danger in democracy, as noted by both ancient and modern theorists such as Aristotle and de Tocqueville is that a regime based on equality for its own sake is led to a subpolitical emphasis on material and bodily things out of its own conception of justice, because the only thing we all have unambiguously in common is the body and its needs. Higher and more intense purposes may persist among individuals and groups, but they are forced out of the public realm of meaning in the interest of equality; hence, the spread of the desire in advanced democracy to "live as one likes," that is, live a private life, whether hedonist or spiritualist. See Leo Strauss, *The City and Man* (Chicago: The University of Chicago Press, 1964), 109–15, for a discussion of Plato's *Republic* in similar terms.

26. Oakeshott, *On Human Conduct*, 183.

27. On the various generalizations of this paragraph, see Machiavelli, *Dis-*

courses on the First Ten Books of Titus Livius, 1, 58; 2, 2; 1, 60; 1, 42; 3, 49, any edition.

28. Machiavelli clearly believed that the success of the Empire, for so long as it lasted, derived from habits and discipline, especially military, acquired under the Republic.

29. Machiavelli, *Discourses*, 1, 4.

30. Polybius, *The Histories*, 6, 15–18.

31. Machiavelli, *Discourses*, 3, 9.

32. Ibid., 3, 1.

33. Ibid., 1, 5–6.

34. Ibid., 2, 3.

35. Ibid., 3, 34.

36. Ibid., 2, 2.

37. David Hume, "Idea of a Perfect Commonwealth," in *Essays, Moral, Political and Literary* (London: Oxford University Press, 1963), 500–1.

38. James Harrington, *The Commonwealth of Oceana*, in *The Political Works of James Harrington*, edited by J. G. A. Pocock (Cambridge: Cambridge University Press, 1977), 272–78.

39. Pocock, *Political Works of James Harrington*, 43.

40. Ibid., 151.

41. Harrington, *Commonwealth of Oceana*, 172.

42. Pocock, *Political Works of James Harrington*, 53.

43. Jean-Jacques Rousseau, *The Social Contract*, 3, 6, any edition.

44. Rousseau, *Emile*, 1, any edition; *The Social Contract*, 3.

45. "Rousseau . . . thought that any experience of change was psychologically debilitating. Change meant uncertainty and upheaval for those who live through it and as such was at all times a source of suffering." Judith Shklar, *Men and Citizens: A Study of Rousseau's Social Theory* (London: Cambridge University Press, 1969), 29.

46. Rousseau, *The Social Contract*, 3, 4.

47. Ibid., 4, 4.

48. Ibid.

49. Ibid.

50. Ibid., 4, 1.

51. For this characterization, see Mary Nichols, *Citizens and Statesmen: A Study of Aristotle's 'Politics'* (Savage, Md.: Rowan & Littlefield Publishers, Inc., 1992), 173–75.

52. Montesquieu, *The Spirit of the Laws*, 3, 3, any edition.

53. For a recent statement of this view, see Skhlar, "Montesquieu and the New Republicanism," in *Machiavelli and Republicanism* edited by G. Bock, Q. Skinner, and M. Viroli (Cambridge: Cambridge University Press, 1990), 265–79.

54. Forrest McDonald, *Novus Ordo Seclorum: The Intellectual Origins of the Constitution* (Lawrence: University of Kansas Press, 1985), 70–77.

55. Ibid., 70–77.

56. Ibid.

57. *Federalist* #14, any edition.

58. *Federalist* #63.

59. On these tensions, see, especially, *Federalist* #37, #51, #60, and #62.

60. *Federalist* #57.

61. *Federalist* #10.

62. *Federalist* #8 and #23.

63. De Tocqueville, *Democracy in America*, 2, 3, 8, any edition.

64. There can be important differences between caring for the common good (or a common object of good) and preserving a system of authority. But, for purposes of our analysis, they have a similar effect in channeling and focusing energy and attention on the problem of the *general context* for political action rather than simply satisfaction of particular interests for their own sake.

65. De Tocqueville, *Democracy in America*, 2, 2, 2.

66. Ibid., 2, 2, 5; 2, 1, 5.

67. Ibid., 2, 3, 26.

68. Ibid., 2, 3, 26.

69. Marvin Meyers, *The Jacksonian Persuasion* (Stanford, Calif.: Stanford University Press, 1957), 74.

70. James Fenimore Cooper, *The American Democrat* (New York, Alfred A. Knopf, 1931), 125.

71. Cooper, *Homeward Bound*, in *Complete Works*, 13 (New York: G. P. Putnams's Sons, 1893), 87–90.

72. Cooper, *American Democrat*, 64–65. Arthur Schlesinger, Jr., makes the same point about the deference of Whig (vs. old Federalist) rhetoric to the values of the "common man," in *The Age of Jackson* (Boston: Little, Brown and Company, 1945), 265–82.

73. "The Republican Form of Government guaranteed for the States reflects the principles of our political way of life or regime. We notice no such explicit guarantee applies to the United States as a whole. . . . Must not the American people as a whole be depended upon to keep the Government of the United States republican? There does not seem to be any other authority available for this purpose." George Anastaplo, *The Constitution of 1787* (Baltimore and London: The Johns Hopkins University Press, 1989), 174.

74. *Cato's Letters* (New York: Russell and Russell Publishers, 1969), 2, #39, "Of the Passions," 49.

75. For an elaborate demonstration on Aristotelian grounds that Wilson and FDR pulled the American political system in the direction of a democracy and away from that of a "mixed regime," see Paul Eidelberg, *A Discourse on Statesmanship: The Design and Transformation of the American Polity* (Urbana: University of Illinois Press, 1974). Against neo-Aristotelians who argue that the United States was never a mixed regime since all branches of government are ultimately connected to popular choice, Eidelberg counters with the argument that this is to confuse efficient with formal causality, and Aristotle meant the latter, that is, a regime mixed of *formal* causes.

76. Woodrow Wilson, *Congressional Government*, 1885, quoted in Eidelberg, *Discourse on Statesmanship*, 279.

77. See, for example, 3–32 of Wilson, *The New Freedom* (New York: Doubleday & Company, 1913); for documentation of Wilson's millennialist side, see Ernest Lee Tuveson, *Redeemer Nation* (Chicago: The University of Chicago Press, 1968), 209–13.

78. Wilson, from *The New Freedom*, quoted in Eidelberg, *Discourse on Statesmanship*, 348 (Emphasis added.)

79. Ibid., 286–87.

80. Ibid.

81. Wilson, "The Study of Administration," in *The Papers of Woodrow*

Wilson, edited by Arthur S. Link 3: 369 (Princeton, N.J.: Princeton University Press, 1968).

82. Ibid., 374.

83. FDR, "The Commonwealth Club Address, 1932," in *The People Shall Judge*, vol. 2, edited by The Staff, Social Sciences I, The College of the University of Chicago (Chicago: The University of Chicago Press, 1949), 449–57.

84. See, in this connection, n. 64.

85. On the general importance of time-conceptions for politics, see the works of Pocock such as *Politics, Language and Time* (New York: Atheneun Publishers, 1973); and *The Machiavellian Movement* (Princeton, N.J.: Princeton University Press, 1975). See, also, my essay, "Liberal Democracy and the Time-Stream," in W. J. Coats, Jr., *The Activity of Politics and Related Essays*, (Selinsgrove, Pa.: Susquehanna University Press, 1989), 150–61. But, whereas Pocock is engaged in the historical exercise of articulating paradigmatic ideas of time for different civilizations or historical epochs, I am engaged in the "unhistorical" exercise of trying to show that in any historical setting there are more and less complex characters afoot, with more and less complicated ideas about time and about what kinds of events in time have meaning; and with more and less influence on political constitutions, which, in turn, affect the time-conceptions of succeeding generations. For an interesting discussion of the connections between the time-conceptions of modern science and modern democracy, see Wyndham Lewis, *Time and Western Man* (New York: Harcourt, Brace and Co., 1928), especially 434–37. What Lewis calls (against the modern "time-philosophy") the "spatializing instinct of man," has similar political effects to what I am calling a cyclical (vs. linear) time-sense.

86. Aristotle, *Politics*, 3, 7.

87. One raised in a democracy, who can still grasp the idea of political authority, is a good candidate for the appelation, "republican"; but the converse does not follow, that is, one born to a monarchy who could grasp the idea of private liberty could imply any number of things.

88. The case of atheistic French republicanism would appear to be the exception which proves the rule. For a comparison of the role of religion in the French and American revolutions, see Patrice Higonnet, *Sister Republics: The Origins of French and American Republicanism* (Cambridge, Mass.: Harvard University Press, 1988), especially 90–95. On the delicate subject of connections between "progressive" democracy and atheism (or at least radically immanentist and pantheist conceptions of deity), see (besides de Tocqueville) Eric Voegelin, *The New Science of Politics* (Chicago and London: The University of Chicago Press, 1952), 143 and 173–178.

89. It might be argued that the only thing in which the republican character specializes is tending to the preservation of a general way of life which will continue to nourish the conditions for the emergence of more of these complex and nonspecialized characters.

90. Quoted in Pocock, *Machiavellian Moment*, 500 n. 95.

91. One could construct other metaphorical axes—for example, subjective and scientifically objective; subjective and collective; and introspective and public. But always, the distinctive characteristic of this personality is the attempt at a commonsensical balance between those extremes which are inescapable. In this particular case, I mean for the metaphor to extend to the intersection of the various "axes" themselves, such that the republican character is attentive *to both the recurring and the general*. That is, it would be

possible to focus on securing recurring appetitive pleasures, or avoiding various bodily threats (e.g., fear of violent death), but these are not *general* conditions, even when extended to populations as a whole. (E.g., provision for the common defense of a system of authority—a general purpose—is not the same as mere provision for the collective avoidance of fear of violent death.) On this reading, then, the human condition is a manageable tension at its best, susceptible to only intermittent moments of resolution. Against this view of moderate tension as a source of health and order, one could cite, on the transcendental side, Plato, and on the immanentist side, a modern democrat such as Wilson; in support of this view, the most obvious source is the ancient Greek Stoic, Chrysippus. See, for example, A. A. Long and D. N. Sedley, eds., *The Hellenistic Philosophers* (Cambridge: Cambridge University Press, 1987) 1:418. For a discussion of democratic political corruption as characterized by the collapse of the tension between major practical polarities such as old and young, male and female, inside and outside, see J. Peter Euben, "Political Corruption in Euripides' *Orestes*, in *Greek Tragedy and Political Theory* edited by Euben (Berkeley: University of California Press, 1986), 236.

92. The point here is that this character be capable of sufficient generalization as to grasp the idea of the political as an architectonic or overarching art, at least in the public dimensions; or, *at a minimum*, that it be capable of seeing the practical utility of political authority. For the curious view that the meaning of something called the "classical republican tradition" was "the supreme value of the intellectual virtues," see Thomas Pangle, *The Spirit of Modern Republicanism* (Chicago: The University of Chicago Press, 1988), chap. 6. Pangle is able to reach such conclusions by strangely searching for the roots of "ancient republicanism" in the idea of Socrates that virtue is knowledge, rather than in Aristotle's discussion of the mixed regime, or in Cicero's discussion of the aims of *res publica* in *De Officiis*. Pangle is silent on all Roman criticism of Greek philosophy, as well as on the Ciceronian affinities of Locke's *Second Treatise*.

93. James Reston, *New York Times*, 11 November 1991, "Adlai & Mario & Ike & George," A11.

94. "In 1908, Arthur F. Bentley fathered the scientific definition of the state as an interest that could be thought of 'as an interest group itself.'" Theodore J. Lowi, *The End of Liberalism: The Second Republic of the United States*, 2d ed. (New York: W. W. Norton & Company, 1979), 37. Lowi then goes on to observe critically against Bentley that "*there is a political context that is not itself competition* within which political competition takes place." (Emphasis added.) This latter statement is characteristic of what I call the "republican outlook."

95. Whether out of philosophical appreciation of the difference between the political and subpolitical; or a sympathetic reading of political history; or habits of deference acquired in families, churches, schools, military service, or elsewhere.

96. *Texas, Petitioner v. Gregory Lee Johnson*, No. 88–155, Decided 21 June 1989, *Criminal Law Reporter*, 6–21–89 45 CRL, 45 CRL 3111. (Emphasis added.)

97. During the Republican National Convention in Dallas in 1984, Gregory Lee Jonson and other protestors burned an American flag in front of the Dallas City Hall while chanting, "America, the red, white, and blue, we spit on you." *Texas, Petitioner v. Gregory Lee Johnson*, 45 CrL 3108.

98. Distinguished from mere "collective" physical well-being.

99. *Halter v. Nebraska*, 205 U.S. 34 (1907), cited in Chief Justice William Rehnquist's dissent, *Texas, Petitioner v. Gregory Lee Johnson*, 45 CrL 3116.

100. *Texas, Petitioner v. Gregory Lee Johnson*, 45 CrL 3119.

101. The original "fighting words" decision is more ambiguous on this question; at issue was a personal insult, but one phrased in political terms ("damn fascist" and "damn racketeer"), *Walter Chuplinsky v. State of New Hampshire* (315 U.S. 568–74), 1942.

102. And, one might add, in its legitimate but obsessive aversion to being manipulated by unscrupulous leaders who employ political abstractions and symbols for self-serving ends.

103. Oakeshott, *On Human Conduct*, 111–15. Oakeshott does imply that there is a difference between a *substantive purpose* (which can be unambiguously accomplished in action and which is used up in being accomplished) and a *general purpose* such as security or moral virtue, which is too general ever to be once and for all achieved, and hence is ongoing by its very nature.

104. For a recent discussion of the scholarly disputes about Locke's influence in prerevolutionary America (as well as a demonstration of his pervasive influence among the New England clergy), see Steven M. Dworetz, *The Unvarnished Doctrine: Locke, Liberalism and the American Revolution* (Durham, N.C.: Duke University Press, 1990), especially 3–38.

105. See, in this connection, Locke's *Second Treatise of Government*, chaps. 5, 7, and 8, any edition.

106. From Locke, *A Letter on Toleration*, quoted in Dworetz, *Unvarnished Doctrine*, 132.

107. For development of this theme, see Dworetz, *Unvarnished Doctrine*, 131–33.

108. Nathan Tarcov, *Locke's Education for Liberty* (Chicago: The University of Chicago Press, 1984), 5. Tarcov's account is slightly misleading on the importance of military duty for Locke. See, in this connection, Thomas Pangle, *The Spirit of Modern Republicanism: The Moral Vision of the American Founders and the Philosophy of Locke* (Chicago: The University of Chicago Press, 1988), 226–27.

109. For a development of this theme, see John Dunn, *The Political Thought of John Locke* (Cambridge: Cambridge University Press, 1969), 214–28.

110. It might be argued that Locke's epistemology as set forth in *An Essay Concerning Human Understanding* helped to lay the basis for such developments in its requirement that revelation be made compatible with laws of instrumental reason and nature. See, for example, Locke, *An Essay Concerning Human Understanding*, vol. 2, edited by A. C. Fraser (New York: Dover Publications, 1959), 425–26. "*Nothing that is contrary to, and inconsistent with, the clear and self-evident dictates of reason, has a right to be urged or asserted to as a matter of faith*. . . ." (Emphasis added.)

111. For a more extensive development of this theme than what is presented here, see my article, "Some Correspondences Between Oakeshott's 'Civil Condition' and the Republican Tradition," in *The Political Science Reviewer* 21 (Spring 1992): 99–115.

112. See, in this context, n. 101.

113. Oakeshott, *On Human Conduct*, 154.

114. Ibid., 183.

115. De Tocqueville, *Democracy in America*, 2, 2, 1.

116. Pocock, *Machiavellian Moment*, 515 and 538.

117. Ibid., 538.

118. Oakeshott, "Rationalism in Politics," in *Rationalism in Politics and Other Essays* (new and exp. ed.), edited by Timothy Fuller (Indianapolis: Liberty Press, 1991), 16–17. For an extended summary of Oakeshott's understanding of modern Rationalism, see my essay, "Michael Oakeshott's Critique of Rationalism in Politics," in W. J. Coats, Jr., *The Activity of Politics and Related Essays*, 34–41.

119. For an application of this insight to actual policy, see my essay, "Liberal Democracy and the Time-Stream: The Case of M.A.D.," in *The Activity of Politics and Related Essays*, 150–62.

120. Allan Bloom, "Justice: John Rawls vs. The Tradition of Political Philosophy," *American Political Science Review* 69 no. 2 (June 1975): 648.

121. John Rawls, "Justice as Fairness: Political not Metaphysical," *Philosophy and Public Affairs* 14, no. 3 (Summer 1985): 227.

122. Rawls, *A Theory of Justice* (The Belknap Press; Cambridge, Mass.: Harvard University Press, 1971), 102.

123. Ibid., 62 and 92.

124. Ibid., 17–19.

125. Here, for example, is a fine statement of the rationale for the Renaissance city-state militia (but one which still does not make all the connections which I wish to draw): "Within this framework, the concept of the militia had a privileged place. Obliging every citizen to bear arms, the militia focused all the conditions of political community. As an institution, it was the country's defence against external enemies, but it also served an important unifying function within the community, the common obligation of military service offsetting the inequality in the roles alotted citizens in civil life. At the same time, the militia required the fulfillment of both the moral and the material conditions of political community. Virtue was a quality citizens needed to display as much in war as in civil affairs, while economic independence was essential if citizens were to be free to take up arms whenever required. Altogether, participation in the militia was the simplest and in the last resort the most important expression of the citizen's political liberty. . . . The bearing of arms might be presented simultaneously as a public duty and a private right, as an expression of the citizen's liberty to participate and as a guarantee of the individual's freedom from authority." John Robertson, *The Scottish Enlightenment and the Militia Issue* (Edinburgh, Scotland: John Donald Publishers, Ltd., 1985), 10 and 12.

126. *Federalist* #23.

127. For a development of this idea, see the third essay of this book, "American Democracy and the Punitive Use of Force."

128. Sir William Blackstone, *Commentaries on the Laws of England*, 11th ed. (London: Strahan and Woodfall, 1791), 3, 3–4; 4, 183–84 (on "preventive defense" in sudden cases).

129. For an easily accessible illustration of the kind of "republican" attitudes I have in mind, see Ralph Peters, *The War in 2020* (New York: Pocket Star Books, 1991), Author's Note. Peters is an active duty army officer and best-selling novelist.

130. In case I have not been sufficiently explicit about the connection between provision of the common defense and *political* equilibrium, let me summarize what has been implied throughout this discussion. Politics, as I understand it, is the moderate and free way of ordering the common part of

our lives together, and reconciling our differences, because it proceeds upon the assumption that human motivations are both rational and irrational (and that there will always be different understandings of what is rational, even in the same body politic). The willingness and capacity to provide for the common defense is a timeless aspect of the truly *political* character (regardless of the likelihood of war at any moment), because it is predicated upon the observation that the causes of war and conflict are both rational and irrational (or, even subconscious), and, hence, preclude exclusive reliance upon the problematic prospect of a perpetual just peace for preservation of the realm of political freedom. For more on this, see my book, *The Activity of Politics and Related Essays* (London and Toronto: Associated University Presses, 1989).

131. To state once more the logical link in this argument: republics are inherently stable regimes because they mix into both their constitutions and the characters of their citizens a complex time-sense granting meaning and importance to *both* recurring (and general) aspects of experience, for instance, constitutional arrangements not easily changed, *and* more transient aspects, for instance, the vicissitudes of the marketplace. They are, then, more likely to avoid the respective dangers to which both autocracy and democracy are prone—failure to deal adequately with the changing in the former case, and equation of the changing with all passage of time, in the latter case.

2

Some Correspondences Between Oakeshott's "Civil Condition" and the Republican Tradition

> *respublica*, a practice of civility specifying . . . conditions to be submitted to in choosing performances, and therefore the common or "public" concern, not the common purpose of *cives*
>
> —Michael Oakeshott, "On the Civil Condition"

The individualist flavor of much of Michael Oakeshott's writing suggests affinities with eighteenth-and nineteenth-century liberalism,[1] yet in his definitive essay on the civil condition he employs Latin words (redolent of Republican Rome) such as *respublica* and *cives* to denote his ideal characters.[2] What correspondence may there be between what might be called the "republican tradition" in European political history and Oakeshott's theoretical and historical account of the European *ethos* of individualism which evolved in the breakup of the medieval realms? And what light, if any, is to be shed in discovering such correspondence?

A brief initial answer to this last question is surely required to justify and guide the rest of the inquiry. There are two sets of advantages to be gained here. One, which I leave to others to pursue, involves the insights to be found in an individualist account of civil obligation which does not even mention the idea of rights, or the priority of rights over duties, but takes its bearings instead from the authority of law. The other advantage, and my interest here, will be to gain insights into the differences between what I call the "republican and democratic characters," and more generally, into certain tendencies of advanced democracies.

I shall proceed by laying out some differences between these two personae as I understand them, and employ Oakeshott's account of the differences between civil and enterprise association in his book, *On Human Conduct*[3] to support and refine some of these differences.

One immediate obstacle to proceeding is the meaning of "republican," and especially the differences between Greek and Roman versions;[4] whether the Greek version is to be traced to Aristotle's mixed regime,[5] or to Socratic intellectual virtue,[6] or directly to Sparta;[7] and the differences between the ancient Greek, Roman, and Renaissance humanist versions of republicanism on the one hand, and more modern versions following Montesquieu, Hume, and the *Federalist* on the other.[8] Since my primary aim *here*[9] is to discover what light Oakeshott's account of civil association may shed on differences between what I am calling the "republican" and "democratic" *personae,* I shall sidestep much of this debate over the meaning of republican, and simply say what I take it to be for the purpose of distinguishing it from democracy.

Taking my bearings from Aristotle's account of the mixed or political regime in Books 3 and 4 of the *Politics,* Cicero's account of *respublica* in *De Officiis,* Machiavelli's account of the Roman republic in the *Discourses* on Livy, and from the *Federalist* (following Pocock's claim that the civic humanist outlook endured in America even as it was dying out in Europe, albeit in a modified form[10]), I suggest that *one* of the distinguishing features of the republican persona is concern for the "common advantage" or "public interest" alongside of, *or as the context for,* particular policies and programs. (Is preservation of this distinction not the logic behind Madison's various institutional contrivances in *Federalist* #10?) The hallmark, then, of this character, is the willingness not merely to live with (as a source of putative "alienation" *à la* Rousseau or Marx) the tension *between* particular political goals *and* concern for the general framework of authority within which they are achieved. Rather, it is the concern to nourish this tension as a discipline for vitality and stability, a concern manifested in, for example, a sense of limits, resistance to extreme specialization in the personality, willingness to serve in the common defense, and so on.[11] And taking my bearings from Plato, Aristotle, de Tocqueville, and some contemporary critics of modern pluralist democracy,[12] I contrast this republican tendency with the democratic tendency to reduce a constitution to a mechanism for the ministration of immediate felt needs, usually physical and material ones, and to exclude or demote concern for formality when it comes to fidelity to authoritative procedures (except where these affect the allocation and distribution of governmental benefits). To put this last point in Platonic terms, democracy is the regime of the body and its needs, because democracy loves equality, and because bodily existence is the one thing we all have in common.[13] Hence, democracy's very conception of fair play or due process leads it over time to define public reality as primarily physical and material.[14]

Now, I believe that Oakeshott's account of civil association in *Human Conduct*, makes an interesting (if oblique) contribution to this discussion in its distinction between civil and enterprise association, as ideal types useful for specifying the character of actual, historic states. Oakeshott distinguishes *between* civil relationship as association in terms of rules as rules, *and* what he calls "enterprise association," or association in terms of the management of the pursuit of a common purpose (or, in some versions, association in which bargainers intermittently transact with one another for *substantive* satisfactions).[15] An example of an enterprise association might be a firehouse, whose purpose is the *substantive* engagement to put out fires, and about whose enterprise we can observe two characteristics which do not appear in civil association. First, while it may have rules of behavior, these rules do not identify the purpose of a firehouse, and might be very similar to the rules of a police station, for example; and, secondly, the substantive purpose is not continuous, but is exhausted in the act of putting out a fire, and is thus dependent on something outside itself for its perpetuation, that is, the occurrence of another fire. Civil association, by contrast, is association in terms of the recognition of general rules as a practice of intercourse, or a common language by analogy, and neither explicitly nor implicitly in terms of accomplishment of substantive purposes, and hence self-sufficient association. It is, in principle, interminable even if it can be, and sometimes is, terminated.

Oakeshott does not actually define what he means by a substantive purpose, but he tells us what it is not—for example, the attempts to achieve security, *tranquillitas*, peace or moral virtue.[16] These, by implication (perhaps following Aristotle's observation in the *Ethics* that action is particular) are too general to be unambiguously accomplished in concrete actions, and hence would appear not to be by themselves either substantive wants or substantive purposes, on Oakeshott's usage. Furthermore, we may observe that a general purpose such as "security" cannot be achieved once and for all, and hence cannot be considered "substantive" in Oakeshott's account, even though the amount of resources a society devoted to such a purpose might be what distinguished it from another society. (Oakeshott's discussion here is reminiscent of the Augustinian theme that a general condition such as contentment is always a by-product of the accomplishment of more specific aims and obligations; as we shall see in a moment, this theme recurs in Oakeshott's critique of modern rationalism.) *Civil* association thus means association in terms of practices of conduct too general to be capable of independently specifying common purposes or substantive wants, and, hence, on Oakeshott's usage, moral rather than instrumental or prudential.[17]

Oakeshott establishes civil association (or *civitas*) as an ideal character by making explicit its logical postulates: it is association in terms of explicitly articulated *rules*, where rules are understood as more general and enduring than commands or directives addressed to identifiable individuals, and requiring particular actions from them as a function of administration);[18] and where rules are also understood as authoritative assertions (vs. theorems or conclusions of reasoning), which call only for consideration in acting, because, in their generality, they are incapable of soliciting specific acts of obedience. "Rules . . . prescribe norms of conduct . . . they cannot tell us what to do or say. . . ."[19] The rules of civil association Oakeshott calls *lex*, and notes that by identifying the basis for association *(civitas)*, *lex* formally relates individuals *(cives)* not otherwise related, "solely in terms of their common recognition of rules which constitute a practice of civility."[20]

Having established civil association as association in terms of practices of authoritative rules incapable of requiring exact performances from its associates, Oakeshott proceeds to derive the other essential institutions and activities logically necessary for such a civil condition. Before following Oakeshott (as expeditiously as possible) through these subsequent derivations, it is fortifying to remind ourselves of why this is interesting, and why we must proceed carefully. The drama of what Oakeshott is doing might be stated thus: in a democratic age, hostile to abstraction, inclined to identify the vocabulary of politics and governance with an enterprise about the concentration of power to distribute substantial benefits to various groups, and to attribute legitimacy to those who can deliver the "goods," Oakeshott is trying to discipline our attention sufficiently long to derive or rejuvenate an entire civil vocabulary from an initial idea of being associated in terms of a "practice of civility," or in terms of the recognition of "rules as rules." There is an added incentive to proceed through this web of abstraction: we might place Oakeshott's account within the context of more well-known accounts in Western political thought, by saying that he proceeds to tell a story about civil freedom which begins from the (anticontractarian) assumption that the freedom to associate or disassociate is not very realistic with regard to comprehensive associations called "states." These are often in practice compulsory to most who inhabit them. Hence, to search for a basis for freedom in contingent acts of choice within a framework of general laws is attractive and realistic. Against Hobbes, Oakeshott will also argue that the freedom of *cives* arises *not* in the *silence*, but in the *generality* of the laws, or terms of association. (In a move which I believe is unique to political theory based upon individualist and nominalist assumptions, this allows Oakeshott to retain the ancient idea of *civitas* as the comprehensive and self-sufficient association, as well as the benefits of logical coherence which flow from this starting point.)

Because of the generality of *lex*, there is another institution postulated by Oakeshott's idea of civil association—a procedure of adjudication for "resolving uncertainties and disputes over how norms of *lex* relate to contingent situations."[21] However, adjudication without enforcement procedures is of little worth; hence, adjudication postulates *ruling* or policing civil association, understood as requiring an "identifiable agent to make a specified choice in an assignable situation.[22] The frequent requirement for new laws postulates legislation, or the authoritative enactment of new *lex;* the requirement for new *lex* postulates an activity conducted in a persuasive (not demonstrative) idiom, involving deliberation and judgment, concerned with the relative desirability of new proposals against old *lex*, and this is, properly speaking, *politics*. But politics is clearly to be distinguished from questions of obligation and authority, the "twin pillars of the civil condition," and the real "public concern" *(respublica)* of *cives*.

> The only understanding of *respublica* capable of evoking the acceptance of all *cives* without exception, and thus eligible to be recognized as the terms of association, is *respublica* understood in terms of its authority.[23]

Thus, for Oakeshott, the civil condition is not association for the pursuit of common purposes, but a "moral condition" concerned with "the terms upon which the satisfaction of wants might be pursued." Hence, in the civil condition, "public" and "private" refer to relationships, not persons and performances, and "they meet in every substantive engagement," the private interest concerned with its success, the public interest concerned with considerations of *lex* in the way it is conducted.[24] (One could say that in persons and performances the concrete relation of public and private comes to light—this is why in actuality they are always mingled.) This condition also postulates *cives* capable both of self-restraint, and the ability to focus their attention so as to be able to pursue their private interests in contingent situations "while thinking in terms of civil intercourse," or "caring for the condition of the civil condition."[25]

To relate all this to something less abstract and more familiar, it is difficult not to be struck by its similarity to Cicero's claim in the second book of *De Officiis* that the republic was lost when the proper distinction between public and private was lost, or to Trenchard's and Gordon's view from the "country" in the name of Cato some eighteen centuries later.

> And though in pursuing Views, Men regard themselves and their own Advantages; yet if they regard the Publick more, or their own in Subservience to the Publick, they may justly be esteemed virtuous and good.[26]

But unlike Cicero or Trenchard and Gordon, Oakeshott is not engaged in practical politics. His is a theoretical enterprise to draw out and make explicit the postulates of a (rare) historical practice; and the "force" of his argument comes in showing the logical (not practical) necessity of understanding *respublica* as a set of general conditions to be observed in every private, substantive engagement, if the meaning of civil freedom as assent to the authority of general laws is not to be contradicted or denied.

To summarize this first and foremost affinity between Oakeshott's account of the civil condition and the republican outlook, I have tried to show that it resides in defending the centrality of the sustained capacity of citizens simultaneously to consider the likely effects of proposed legislation and policy both for their own private interests, and for the authoritative context or system of general laws and practices within which their substantive interests are pursued. The very "amateurishness" of this orientation makes it republicanlike in providing resistance to extreme specialization in the personality directed exclusively toward securing substantive success in specific enterprises or activities.

A second correspondence (or affinity) between Oakeshott's account of the civil obligations of individuals and the republican tradition is the emphasis on what he calls the historic European disposition (of individual human beings since at least the Italian Renaissance) to be distinct, to "live a life for a man like me." I want now to try to show that, despite differences in emphasis, this *ethos* is consistent with, or friendly toward, the practice of republican deference, in a way that it is not consistent with the idea of democratic equality of conditions described, for example, by de Tocqueville in the second volume of *Democracy in America*. "But for equality, their passion is ardent, insatiable, incessant, invincible." Pocock has argued, in a discussion of the effects of the republican tradition in America, that "deference was not a hierarchical but a republican characteristic," arising in the respect different kinds of people held for different kinds of virtues and talents, permitting the individual to know himself "through the respect shown by his fellows for the qualities publicly recognized in him,"[27] and distinguished from the democratic developments toward conformity and uniformity de Tocqueville was beginning to observe in Jacksonian America.

> But once men were, or it was held that they ought to be all alike, his only means of self-discovery lay in conforming to everybody's notions of what he ought to be and was. This produced a despotism of opinion, since nothing but diffused general opinion now defined the ego or its standards of judgment.[28]

It is interesting here to compare Pocock's discussion of deference (as found in Harringtonian and neo-Harringtonian republicanism) with Oakeshott's treatment of Montesquieu's hypothetical constitutions in *De l'esprit des lois*. Oakeshott makes it clear that what Montesquieu calls a "republic," distinguished by the principle of "virtue," would not qualify as civil association but rather as a corporation aggregate in its Spartan-like attempt to educate and manage the lives of its citizens around a common substantive idea of the common good, and a renunciation of each's own self *(soi-meme)*.[29] Rather, it is the ideal-type Montesquieu names "monarchy" which Oakeshott sees as the closest (among Montesquieu's three ideal constitutions) to civil association, and this because "it is association in respect of fidelity to one another in terms of a system of rules of conduct," in which "every enterprise is 'private' and none is immune from the 'public' considerations specified in *la loi*," and because Montesquieu himself implied that it best accommodated "the dominant moral disposition of the inhabitants of modern Europe: the historic disposition to be 'distinct.'"[30] Oakeshott also goes on to suggest that civil association has affinities with the political visions of, among others, Machiavelli, Locke, Sidney, Burke, Madison, Benjamin Constant, and de Tocqueville.[31] One might observe in passing that in the context of North American republicanism, Oakeshott's views may be seen as *more congenial* to what Forrest McDonald calls the "tobacco plantation country" version, characterized by a "leisure ethic," personal independence, and strict attention to the structure of political institutions as the basis for liberty, *than to* the puritanical New England and Southern Baptist versions of republicanism and their emphasis on personal moral rectitude as the basis for "public virtue."[32]

To summarize, my point here is that Oakeshott's account of the *ethos* of the individual which evolved in the breakup of the medieval realms, an *ethos* to cultivate the freedom (to choose) inherent in moral agency, can be at home in a situation of what Pocock calls republican deference, in a way it cannot be at home within a democratic *ethos* of equality of conditions, where all are assumed to want basically the same things, and, hence, to be always in competition with one another, even if in the name of "human solidarity." Thus, a second affinity with republicanism in Oakeshott's account of the civil condition lies in the correspondence of the individualist desire to be distinct with the deference shown in republics to a genuine diversity of talents and callings—for example, the kind of deference shown in America to a natural aristocracy of political talent prior to Jacksonian democracy, and not much apparent since.[33] One might also extend the argument to suggest that the desire to be distinct and self-reliant leads away from the extreme civic and psychic dependence upon one another and *upon strong leaders*, censured by republican critics of democracy from Thucydides to opponents of the New Deal.

There is yet a third correspondence in Oakeshott's work with republicanism, but to show it I must move outside of the essays in *Human Conduct*, and back to his earlier writings on modern rationalism and the antidotes for its excesses. It has to do with seeing clearly the things which make up a human life, and with avoiding political illusions. It also has affinities to the idea of republican balance in the face of urbane contrivances to expand

and expand the realm of things which can be defined as solely what conventional opinion says they are. What I have in mind may be illustrated by Pocock's characterization of the "country Whig" critique of the corrupting eighteenth-century enterprise to create wealth primarily through credit.

> Virtue must involve the cognition of things as they really were; the power of Credit was irredeemably subjective and it would take all the authority of society to prevent her from breaking loose to submerge the world in a flood of fantasy . . . the individual would exist . . . only at the fluctuating value imposed upon him by his fellows. . . .[34]

Or, one might look to the educational writings of Rousseau on the illusions of cities which confused the theater and role-playing with civic life, and required the perspective of the country to regain balance. Or, for a more contemporary illustration of this kind of critique one might look to some of the literature of the past two decades concerning the illusions involved in the disastrous American attempt to apply the hypothetical logic of academic, nuclear deterrence theory to actual guerrilla warfare in Southeast Asia.[35] Or, finally, for perhaps the best-known illustration of the blindnesses of which compounded urbane opinion is capable, one might simply recall Hans Christian Andersen's story of the emperor's "new clothes." What is common to all of these examples is the urbane tendency to equate conventional opinion with all of reality, or reality outside the city's walls.

Now my point here is that much of Oakeshott's critique of the modern world of the past three and a half centuries is a version of the view that it is not seeing clearly or impartially, evident in his liking for the French expression, *autres temps, autres folies;* and, in addition, that this desire to see clearly, to grasp firmly the structure of political reality, is also the source of the republican claim to independence and hence stability in time, and, hence, another "republican affinity" in Oakeshott's thought. This last point about republics has been especially developed in Pocock's *Machiavellian Moment,* but it is implicit in the idea of civic corruption in old cities and advanced democracies as a form of extreme dependence on the opinion of one another which leads to myopic vision, or to the belief that the city's opinion is a power that can "master the universe." (Given the power of public opinion in democracy, this problem is compounded in democratic urbane life.)

Consider briefly Oakeshott's critique of modern rationalism in this context: Rationalism Oakeshott indicts as a vulgarization of some of the ideas of Bacon and Descartes, which issued in a belief about the sovereignty of technique in practical affairs. It is characterized by the desire for certainty and control; by the belief in distinct beginning and ending points; and by belief in the universal applicability of its techniques. But, in fact, Rationalism's approach to knowledge and practice is illusory.

> The superiority of technical knowledge lay in its appearance of springing from pure ignorance and ending in certain and complete knowledge. . . . But, in fact, this is an illusion. As with every other sort of knowledge, learning a technique does not consist of getting rid of pure ignorance, but in reforming knowledge which was already there . . . technical knowledge is never, in fact, self-complete. . . . And if its self-completeness is illusory, the certainty . . . is also an illusion.[36]

According to Oakeshott, Rationalism's major error is to misperceive the nature of practical skill, a skill which arises in the fluidity of each craft's own distinctive form and content ("the poetic character of all human activity"[37]), a fluidity ruptured in the misguided and impatient Rationalist attempt to abstract a technique from one concrete activity (e.g., marketing), put it in a book, and apply it universally to other activities (e.g., politics or war).

> The new man, lately risen to power, will often by found throwing away his book and relying upon his general experience . . . as a business man or trade union official . . . but still, it is not a knowledge of the political traditions of his society. . . .[38]

This illusion, in turn, leads to modern versions of the "Tower of Babel" which misperceive the limits of politics, leading political practitioners to an attempt to satisfy by political means substantive needs (including psychic ones) that is not, in the nature of things, possible. Oakeshott says that when Rationalism invades political and moral life, it is characterized by a problem-solving attitude, directed by "felt needs" interpreted by techniques or abridgments called ideologies (or moral codes).[39] In his discussion of "felt needs" Oakeshott might appear to be getting close to a critique of what may be called "democratic passions," but we must be careful here given his resistance to general political explanations. "Felt needs" turn out to be irritations generated by abstractions (the gap between the code and the current situation), rather than by genuine concrete knowledge.

> Book in hand . . . the politicians of Europe pore over the simmering banquet they are preparing . . . but their knowledge does not extend beyond the written word which they read mechanically . . . it generates ideas in their heads but no tastes in their mouths.[40]

Perhaps the most that can be said in linking Oakeshott's criticism of Rationalism and his account of civil and enterprise association is that the prevalence of the illusory belief in the sovereignty of political technique to satisfy substantive wants, makes it more difficult to gain a hearing for the idea of *respublica* as a practice of authority, rather than a corporation aggregate to exploit as efficiently as possible the resources of the earth, with no need for a vocabulary of obligation detached from concerns of practical management.

To follow up this last point, the understanding of human balance and civic balance as a tension between formal and substantive considerations is obscured by the prevalence of practical discourse and activity directed solely toward the practical. Although Oakeshott would hardly condone so "unhistorical" a comparison, it is difficult not to observe that his critique of the errors of modern Rationalism, the Baconian project in general, and the view of the state as an "enterprise association," all can be taken as a particular historical version of the old Socratic insight that the vocabulary of politics and justice arises in a complex interaction of both formal and substantive considerations, and is rendered superfluous when applied to substantive or subpolitical considerations solely. At any rate, this is my understanding of the reason why Socrates, Glaucon, and Adeimantus must build increasingly complex cities (in words) before they can identify justice in the dialogues of Plato's *Republic*—because it is only in the more complex cities that there is a sufficiently complex interplay between formal and substantive considerations as to require a relatively high-order abstraction such as "justice" to describe it.

To summarize this third "republican affinity" in Oakeshott's thought, I have tried to show that Oakeshott's critique of modern Rationalism has parallels with republican critiques of democracies and cities, which systematically exclude from public discussion insights of the countryside, over time distorting political reality at the expense of political and related skills. Foremost among these parallels is a critique of the illusory belief that what was a certain and self-contained technique or ideology was, in fact, partial and incapable of standing on its own.

There is one last theme in Oakeshott's discussion of civil association which is interesting from the standpoint of republicanism, especially its requirement for citizens capable of separating questions of authority from those of substantive interests. This is Oakeshott's treatment of morality. Oakeshott, we saw earlier, considers civil association to be association in terms of *moral* conditions because it is association in terms of laws and practices of authority too general to be construed as instrumental to, or prudential for, the satisfaction of specific, substantive wants in preestablished, identifiable acts.[41] Such a treatment of morality has some structural similarities with the Kantian categorical imperative, and perhaps with Rousseau's "general will," but there are crucial differences. Oakeshott's *civis* is a being *divided* between loyalties to the success of his substantive interests, and loyalties to the practice of civility within which they are pursued. There is here no frequent hope as in the Ciceronian and Rousseuan accounts, of an identification of the public and private interests; nor is there any "dialectic" idea, as in the Rousseuan and Kantian accounts, that we are "free" in obeying a law which we give to ourselves. Rather, for Oakeshott, the chance to practice morality arises in the ability to distinguish formal from substantive considerations, while holding them in tension without the misplaced desire to see the tension permanently resolved. Similarly, the preservation of civil freedom depends on the continued widespread ability to separate formal issues of legitimacy from the satisfaction of substantive wants. In this last sense, Oakeshott's account of civil association is certainly consistent with republican traditions of mutual deference among a genuine diversity of talents, distinguished from the more democratic view that we are all characterized by the same basic wants, hence basically equal, hence "political" only in our mutual strivings for position within the "group solidarity."

Perhaps Oakeshott might be viewed, within the context of this essay's concerns, as a kind of classical liberal (a residual medievalist even) who tried to account for individual freedom in terms of Roman ideas about obligations to the authority of law rather than Greek ideas about the development of personality—which latter ideas, when combined with modern millennialist ideas of social and historical progress,[42] have produced political theories no longer especially friendly to the freedom of either individuals or republics.

1991

Notes

1. For a development of this, see, for example, Wendell J. Coats, Jr., "Michael Oakeshott as Liberal Theorist," *Canadian Journal of Political Science* 18, no. 4 (December 1985): 773–87; and Paul Franco, *The Political Philosophy of Michael Oakeshott* (New Haven, Conn.: Yale University Press, 1990). See, also, Alan Ryan, "Hobbes and Individualism," in *Perspectives on Thomas Hobbes*, edited by G. A. J. Rogers and Alan Ryan, 105 (Oxford: Clarendon Press, 1988).

2. Oakeshott says explicitly that he is employing "somewhat archaic" expressions to denote ideal characters when possible, to avoid confusion with their current historic counterparts [*On Human Conduct* (Oxford: Clarendon Press, 1975), 109]. Nevertheless, we may observe that these are Roman, not Greek, "archaic" expressions; that in spite of disclaimers, the rhetorical effect of these expressions is still felt; and, finally, that Oakeshott has written elsewhere of the Roman genius for ruling, in "The Rule of Law," in *On History and Other Essays* (Oxford: Basil Blackwell, 1983), 164. See, also, on Oakeshott's view of the Romans, Maurice Cranston, "In Memoriam: Michael Oakeshott, 1901–1990," *Political Theory* 19, no. 3 (August 1991). 326.

3. Most of this discussion is contained in the center essay of *Human Conduct*, "On the Civil Condition." Some of it is also in the third essay, "On the Character of a Modern European State."

4. For a discussion, see Quentin Skinner, "The Republican Ideal of Political Liberty," in *Machiavelli and Republicanism*, edited by G. Bock, Q. Skinner, and M. Viroli, 291–309. (Cambridge: Cambridge University Press, 1990).

5. For this view, see Paul Eidelberg, *A Discourse on Statesmanship: The Design and Transformation of the American Polity* (Urbana: University of Illinois Press, 1974); and Leslie G. Rubin, "The Republic of Aristotle: Politics and the Best Regime" (Ph.D. diss., Boston College, University Microfilms International, 1985, especially, Introduction, sec. B, "The Political Virtues of Middle-Class Rule," 4–11. This is also my own view—that "republic" makes a meaningful distinction when used to denote Aristotle's "generic" or mixed regime of "middling" citizens capable of the common defense. For a recent assertion of the "sociological" view that this is a meaningless distinction, see Josiah Ober, *Mass and Elite in Democratic Athens* (Princeton, N.J.: Princeton University Press, 1989), 30 n. 70.

6. For this rather unusual view, see Thomas L. Pangle, *The Spirit of Modern Republicanism* (Chicago: The University of Chicago Press, 1988).

7. See, for example, Elizabeth Rawson, *The Spartan Tradition in European Thought* (London: Oxford University Press, 1969).

8. For a discussion, see Judith Shklar, "Montesquieu and the New Republicanism," in *Machiavelli and Republicanism*, edited by G. Bock, Q. Skinner, and M. Viroli, 265–79. See, also Marizio Viroli, "The Concept of *Ordre* and the Language of Classical Republicanism in Jean-Jacques Rousseau," in *The*

Languages of Political Theory in Early-Modern Europe, edited by Anthony Pagden, especially 165 (Cambridge: Cambridge University Press, 1987).

9. See the title essay for an exploration of some issues of this debate.

10. J. G. A. Pocock, *The Machiavellian Moment: Forentine Political Thought and the Atlantic Republican Tradition* (Princeton, N.J.: Princeton University Press, 1975), 506–52.

11. It should be clear that I am *not* employing "republic" in Rousseau's sense of a simple and undivided Spartan-like devotion to the common good; this orientation or habituation seems to me to be more accurately described as "aristocratic."

12. "There is a political context that is not itself competition, within which competition takes place." Theodore J. Lowi, *the End of Liberalism*, 2d ed. (New York: W. W. Norton & Company, 1979), 37.

13. This is my understanding of one of the implications of Books 7 and 8 of Plato's *Republic*. See, also, on this point, Leo Strauss, *The City and Man* (Chicago: The University of Chicago Press, 1964), 109–15.

14. This is my understanding of one of de Tocqueville's recurrent themes in *Democracy in America*. See, for example, 2, 2, 11, "Peculiar Effects of the Love of Physical Gratifications in Democratic Times," any edition.

15. Oakeshott, *On Human Conduct*, 111–15.

16. Ibid., 119.

17. Ibid., 122.

18. Ibid., 124–125.

19. Ibid., 126.

20. Ibid., 128.

21. Ibid., 131.

22. Ibid., 141.

23. Ibid., 154.

24. Ibid., 146.

25. Ibid., 177 and 186.

26. *Cato's Letters* (New York: Russell and Russell, 1969), 2, #39, "Of the Passions," 49.

27. Pocock, *Machiavellian Moment*, 515 and 538.

28. Ibid., 538.

29. Oakeshott, *On Human Conduct*, 247.

30. Ibid., 250–51.

31. Ibid., 244–46.

32. Forrest McDonald, *Novus Ordo Seclorum: The Intellectual Origins of the Constitution* (Lawrence: University of Kansas Press, 1985), 73–75.

33. See, for example, the characterization of Whig vs. old Federalist rhetoric in Arthur Schlesinger, Jr., *The Age of Jackson* (Boston: Little, Brown and Company, 1945), 265–82.

34. Pocock, *Machiavellian Moment*, 437 and 464.

35. See, for example, my essay, "Liberal Democracy and the Time-Stream: The Case of M.A.D.," in Wendell J. Coats, Jr., *The Activity of Politics and Related Essays* (Selinsgrove, Pa: Susquehanna University Press, 1989), 150–62.

36. Michael Oakeshott, "Rationalism in Politics," in *Rationalism in Politics and Other Essays* (new and exp. ed.), edited by Timothy Fuller (Indianapolis: Liberty Press, 1991), 16–17; for a more extensive summary of Oakeshott's understanding of modern Rationalism, see my essay, "Michael Oakeshott's Cri-

tique of Rationalism in Politics," in *Activity of Politics and Related Essays*, 34–41.

37. Oakeshott, *Rationalism in Politics*, 479.

38. Ibid., 35–36.

39. For Oakeshott's discussion of "Rationalist morality," see the 1949 essay, "The Tower of Babel," in *Rationalism in Politics*, 465–87.

40. Oakeshott, *Rationalism in Politics*, 27.

41. Oakeshott, *On Human Conduct*, 122.

42. For a discussion of millennialist tendencies in the United States, see the classic work by Ernest Lee Tuveson, *Redeemer Nation* (Chicago: The University of Chicago Press, 1968).

3

American Democracy and the Punitive Use of Force: Requiem for the McNamara Model

> In exacting penalties . . . this must be observed particularly, that war is not to be waged on such a pretext against him whose forces are equal to our own. For, as in the case of a civil judge, he who wishes to avenge crimes by armed force ought to be much more powerful than the other party.
>
> —Grotius, *On the Law of War and Peace* 2, 24, sec. 7

Introduction

In a blistering public indictment of the Reagan administration's naval policies in the Persian Gulf, former Secretary of the Navy James Webb wrote the following lines:

> The administration chose a minimal course of retaliation against Iran, one that in itself could neither have deterred the Iranians nor insulated our sailors from further actions by Iran. . . . The administration carefully nurtured the notion of "proportional response" with respect to our Persian Gulf activities.[1]

This description of the minimal use of force in punitive threat and retaliation to deter conventional force attacks is reminiscent of the McNamara approach to the conduct of the Vietnam war. In combination with the way U.S. Marines were used in Lebanon in 1983, and with changes in this administration's appoach to its own strategic defense program, these words of former Secretary Webb direct attention to the issue of the continued influence of the McNamara Defense Department and its advisers.

The aim of this study is to investigate whether, or to what extent and where, a model for the use of armed force developed by McNamara and his advisers, is still exerting influence and control over U.S. policy and outlook. Constructed in the context of mutual nuclear deterrence, the model claims to have relevance for all operational levels down to "low-intensity" conflict and counterterroism, and was used to prosecute the Vietnam War.[2] The essence of the model, as exposited in 1966 by its most exemplary theorist, Harvard economist Tom Schelling,[3] is to skip the stage of military victory and use increments of pain infliction for direct political bargaining, without disarming the enemy. The argument is made that such an approach to the use of force is necessary in the nuclear age to protect national interests by securing mutual accommodation through manipulation and control of the risks of escalation to deter and compel adversaries, by punitive retaliation, or its threat, but without resort to war itself.[4]

Yet there are recognized problems with this approach to the use (and forbearance of the use) of armed force. At the level of nuclear deterrence, the model embodies a fundamental contradiction—the attempt to use the dangers of escalation into higher conflict to induce bargaining and coerce opponents, while also continuing to eliminate the very same risks which are the real deterrent to further aggression. I have dealt with this problem at length elsewhere,[5] and will not take it further here. But the model has other problems at the level of guerrilla warfare and low-intensity conflict (as became unambiguously evident during the Vietnam War), both vis-à-vis opponents and a government's own domestic political support. This monograph is an attempt to set out the logic of the McNamara model; show that it really was *the* controlling factor, insofar as U.S. policy is concerned, in both the Cuban missile crisis and the Vietnam War; show its effects on our decision to use force "incrementally" in Vietnam, and on subsequent public opinion; and investigate whether the outlook of the model still obtains at policy and operational levels, regardless of the use (or not) of its explicit language.

The Model

It is not necessary to summarize everything ever written about, or in justification of, the approach to the use of force I am calling the McNamara-Schelling model.[6] For our purposes, it is sufficient to describe its operational requirements and implications. Schelling's major assertion is that given the dangers of escalation into nuclear conflict, armed force (or its threat) must now be used only "punitively" as a form of direct political bargaining, skipping the traditional military stage to disarm opponents. In Schelling's own words, "military strategy can no longer be thought of . . . as the science of military victory." Instead, the "instruments of war" have now become primarily "punitive" and military strategy has become "the diplomacy of violence," concerned with "coercion, intimidation and deterrence," and grounded in the ability to make "someone afraid to assault you," through the "bargaining power" to "hurt . . . inflict pain and grief. . . ." And to situate all of this in U.S. strategic history, Schelling tells us that his patron, "Secretary McNamara was proposing a new approach to warfare in a new era, an era in which the power to hurt is more impressive than the power to oppose.[7]

The points of operational interest in the model for the punitive use of force are the following:

1. It attempts to induce bargaining independent of the ability to control, contain or disarm the opponent.
2. Thus, it proceeds openly, slowly, incrementally, and intermittently (as in the bombing of North Vietnam prior to 1972),
3. It views the use of all firepower primarily as a matter of targeting and destruction, rather than as an aspect of the tactical arts of ward off, close with, and disarm enemy attacks as operational steps on the way to restoration of orderly peace.
4. It views all use of threat of force in terms of an "escalatory continuum" in which the theat of escalation into higher levels of destruction is manipulated in such a way that adversaries are expected to constrain themselves through "economically rational" calculations about break-even points in the give-and-take of pain infliction (destruction) or its threat.

By way of further delineation of the model, it is instructive to note its differences from two older (but non-Clausewitzean) military concepts. The model differs from ideas of theorists of air power on population bombing, and from the idea of attrition warfare, in its aversion to the use of *shock* in obtaining military and political goals. Incapacitating shock, understood as the breakdown of patterns of order (whether in individuals or in political systems as a whole), had always been viewed as a necessary and limiting component of any use of force. In brief, it permits the defeat of opponents short of their entire destruction. But two aspects of shock generation contradict assumptions of the McNamara-Schelling model for coercive bargaining and crisis management in the nuclear age. Shock requires concentrated, overwhelming, and decisive use of force, and it incapacities opponents making them systemically incapable of further "economic" rationality and control over themselves and their own military forces. Hence, it might lead, according to the model, to uncontrollable escalation, even apparently in low- and midintensity conflict, to judge by our conduct of the Vietnam War. The aim of the model is always to use the threat of further pain infliction as an incentive for "rational" bargaining, rather than to induce incapacitating shock in opponents. And, in this regard, it differs from even Hans Delbrueck's attrition warfare ("Ermattungs-strategie"), which was still intended to incapacitate or exhaust enemy forces as a step on the way to disarming them, and could include, for example, steps for the serious interdiction or blockade of enemy supply routes, or destruction of its economy.[8]

The Model and the Cuban Missile Crisis

To see the model being applied in action by McNamara, we need only turn to the now (mostly) public transcript of the 27 October 1962 meetings of the Executive Committee (ExComm) of the National Security Council (NSC) during the Cuban missile crisis.[9] It becomes readily apparent that McNamara was operating explicitly from the canons of this abstract model of "coercive diplomacy." To show this, it is necesary to relate the remarks of McNamara at some length, and to some extent, those of President Kennedy. Although Kennedy never argued in such abstract terms as McNamara, it becomes apparent that he was taking his bearings from a scenario in his own mind about a major escalation of hostilities in Europe and elsewhere. The only member of the ExComm to argue explicitly with McNamara's general assumptions was CIA Director John McCone, and he was consistently and politely ignored, as we shall see.

In the course of the ExComm discussion, several issues recurred. One was whether to withdraw our Jupiter missiles in Europe as part of a deal for the Soviets to withdraw their missiles from Cuba; another was the likely reaction of NATO and especially Turkey, to such a deal; another was whether to keep surveillance over Cuba after a U.S. U–2 aircraft was downed by a

SAM missile; and yet another was whether to take military action against Cuba or isolated targets in Cuba. McNamara's general approach to all these questions was to lay out a series of hypotheticals based on "our action-their reaction" into higher levels of escalation. When Kennedy left the room, McNamara finally began to raise the specter of escalation into all-out nuclear war. Three things are apparent in what McNamara was doing: (1) his overriding goal was always "crisis stability" at any cost (i.e., he was prepared to err on any side but that); (2) his hypothetical escalation scenarios were meant primarily to "sober up" and constrain his own fellow advisers, not to serve as real alternatives for action; and (3) his scenarios always proceeded on the basis of the "worst case" hypothesis rather than on objective assessments of what the Soviets might likely do. But let the reader judge from the following remarks:

> *McNamara.*
> Mr. President, I wonder if we should not take certain actions with respect to the Jupiters in Turkey and Italy *before* we act in Cuba. . . . If we act in Cuba, the only way we can act now is with full attack. I don't think we can make any limited attacks when they're shooting at our reconnaissance aircraft. . . . If we send . . . sorties in against Cuba, we must be prepared to follow-up with an invasion in about . . . days. If we start out on that kind of a program, it seems to me the Soviets are very likely to feel forced to reply with military action someplace, particularly if these missiles—Jupiter missiles—are still in Turkey. . . .[10]

At this point it is clear that McNamara had reached the conclusion that we could take no action against Cuba (e.g., limited air strikes) short of all-out invasion, and we could not do that until we had solved the problem of U.S. missiles in Turkey, since the Soviets might attack there or elsewhere (e.g., Berlin). After further discussion, the president basically accepted this reasoning, and it seemed to accord with his own fears about general escalation.

> *JFK.*
> The escalation is going on, and we think this is very likely, that there would be some reprisal against possibly Turkey and possibly against Berlin. . . . What we're going to be faced with is . . . maybe we'll have to invade or make a massive strike on Cuba which may lose Berlin. That's what concerns me.[11]

McNamara next introduced his "model" when reports came

into the ExComm that a U.S. U–2 reconnaissance plane had been downed by a SAM missile.

> *McNamara.*
> We had fire on the surveillance . . . are we going to send surveillance flights in? And I think we have basically two alternative(s). Either we decide not to send them in at all or we decide to send them in with proper cover. If we send them in with proper cover and they're attacked, we must attack back, either the SAMs and/or MIG aircraft that comes against them, or the ground fire that comes up. . . .[12]

At this time, Kennedy left the room, and McNamara took charge of the meeting. In what followed, we must rely on the editor's summaries of the minutes, but they are quite explicit—McNamara now raised the specter of escalation into catastrophic nuclear war. It is obvious that McNamara is going through the steps of an abstract model of crisis management, and in his mind at least, the *major* object was to deter any conceivable avenue toward higher escalation, not the Soviets or their aims in Cuba. As he himself later said to the editors of the Excomm transcripts, "If you keep your mind focused on the potential adverse consequences in a situation like the Cuba missile crisis, then . . . you must focus first and foremost on the *possible* catastrophe and see to it that you do nothing to raise the risk of its occurrence."[13] This was clearly McNamara's intent in the following events summarized by the editor:

> McNamara takes charge of the meeting and proposes a verbal exercise . . . the point is that if the U.S. attacks Soviet nuclear missiles in Cuba, and the Soviets respond against our NATO ally in Turkey, we very likely will find ourselves in a catastrophic nuclear war. . . . The effect of McNamara's exercise is evidently quite electrifying. Many ExComm members appear to believe that McNamara is saying that . . . nuclear war is becoming increasingly *probable*.[14]

McNamara went on again to establish his hypothetical linkages precluding any immediate action against Cuba, since the Soviets might attack the Jupiter missiles in Turkey, or attack elsewhere in NATO, forcing us into all-out invasion of Cuba, which might escalate into catastrophic nuclear war. The only member of the ExComm who challenged McNamara at the Level of the presuppositions of his entire model was CIA Director John McCone who said that we should stop trying to *negotiate* over the latest escalation (the downing of our U–2) and confront Khrushchev.

> *McCone.*
> I think that we ought to . . . send directly to Khrushchev by fast wire the most violent protest . . . that he stop this business . . . right away, or we're going to take out those SAM-sites *immediately*.[15]

McCone's suggestion was politely ignored.

Two subsequent occurrences are germane here. The editor of the transcript speculates that the "real value" of a visit by Robert Kennedy to Soviet Ambassador Anatoly Dobrynin "may have been to strike the same fear of uncontrollable war into the Soviets that the previous ExComm discussion, initiated by McNamara, had struck into many ExComm members themselves."[16] And, some of McNamara's last words on the October 27 transcript are also telling from the standpoint of the model's logic.

> *McNamara.*
> I would say only that we ought to keep some kind of pressure on . . . tomorrow night, that indicates we're (serious?). . . . I believe we should issue an order tonight calling up the twenty-four air reserve squadrons, roughly 300 troop carrier transports. . . .[17]

The point here is that Secretary of Defense McNamara was never thinking in terms of requirements of any military mission, but again and always using the threat of increased and uncontrollable escalation (while at the same time doing everything possible to lessen this threat) in order to determine actions *of either side* which in his view might threaten "crisis stability." In other words, he was using the threat of imagined or future pain and destruction (brought on by one's own actions) as the basis for inducing negotiations.

It is also clear, I believe, that both McNamara and Kennedy were viewing the entire confrontation through the lens of a model or scenario for hypothetical alternatives collapsing into an all-out escalation of conflict around the globe. Kennedy may have been reacting more in terms of his understanding of events leading to the First World War as described by Barbara Tuchman's *Guns of August*,[18] and McNamara more in terms of an academic model, but neither was attempting to make a judgment about likely Soviet reactions based on the current military situation and past Soviet behavior. Rather (with Kafkaesque vengeance) the entire ExComm drama unfolded in a reality composed largely of thoughts of *our* own creation, and thoughts widely divergent from the objective military situation.

I do not wish to sidetrack this investigation by moving into a consideration of whether we could simply have dominated the entire situation, but in support of the last assertion, I will simply relate the views of high-ranking air force generals at the time of which the following is typical:

> *General Burhinal.*
> We had, not supremacy, but complete nuclear superiority over Soviets. . . . We could have written our own book at that time, but our politicians did not understand what happens when you have such a degree of superiority as we had, or they simply didn't know how to use it. They were busily engaged in saving face for the Soviets and making concessions . . . when all we had to do was write our own ticket.[19]

And, on the same point, in a recent article on Soviet views of the incident, Raymond Garthoff relates the following:

> An American intelligence report from a "reliable well-placed" Soviet source received about 6 months after the crisis said that a very secret Central Committee directive issued during the crisis stated that the Soviet Union would not go to war over Cuba even if the United States invaded Cuba. The report . . . has never been confirmed or denied.[20]

The Model and the Vietnam War

The McNamara model for the punitive use of armed force can account for our general operational conduct of the Vietnam War. Although commanders were permitted to use force decisively in local encounters, this was not permitted at a theater level, or for air and naval warfare. Up until the end of the Nixon presidency, force was used incrementally in the context of the threat of escalation as an inducement to bargaining (i.e., "to convince the enemy he could not win"), and it was not used until 1972 in such a way as to induce systemic disorder or shock in the North Vietnamese. Much has been written in analysis of our conduct of the war, and addressing some of the more penetrating analysis is a quick and convincing way of demonstrating the application of the McNamara model at the highest levels, even after McNamara departed the office of Secretary of Defense. I will proceed by summarizing two published accounts of the war which coincide with part of my own analysis, but which stop short of drawing the connections with the entire McNamara model for the punitive use of force against the backdrop of escalation into nuclear war (which, of course, the model never intends to permit). I will then try to show that at the places where these books simply stop, or stop examining assumptions, the canons of the model provide the most satisfactory explanation of our general conduct of the war.

A good point of departure for a comprehensive analysis of our conduct of the war is a recent book by a career foreign service officer stationed in Hawaii and Thailand for much of the war. Norman Hannah's *Key to Failure: Laos and the Vietnam War* (Foreword by Col. Harry Summers)[21] draws heavily on Hannah's own memorandums at the time, and also spans both diplomatic and military considerations, rising to the level of an informed general account. Hannah's thesis follows. The outcome of the Vietnam War can be explained as the consequence of a "conceptual 'process' he calls 'incrementalism'," which "formed the common denominator of our decision-making, military and civilian, throughout the war," and which he defines as "the practice of reducing big choices into small incremental bits," "without facing directly the ultimate big decision to which they led." In this case, they led, according to Hannah, to our refusal to isolate the battle area by cutting off the Ho Chi Minh trail through southern Laos, out of observance of the 1962 Geneva Accords on Laos which the North Vietnamese continuously violated. In the end, the United States "incrementally split the difference between defending South Vietnam and not defending it." Hannah also notes that his focus is "on the 'how' of incrementalism . . . the "why" is beyond the scope of this effort."[22] I believe the "why" is to be found in the McNamara model which includes the idea of coercive incremental pressures applied up to the point of threatening "crisis stability." Consider its explanatory power in the following instances, where it is apparent that McNamara is operating from the same model of hypothetical linear escalation as he operated from in the Cuban missile crisis. Hannah cites the following from a December 1965 McNamara memorandum:

> If the U.S. were willing to commit enough forces—perhaps 600,000 or more—we could ultimately prevent North Vietnam and the Vietcong from sustaining conflict at a significant level. When this point

was reached, however, the question of Chinese intervention would become critical. . . .

It follows, therefore, that the odds are about even that, even with the recommended deployments, we will be faced in early 1967 with a military stand-off at a much higher level, with pacification still stalled, and with any prospect of success marred by the chances of active Chinese intervention.[23]

Hannah then raises some questions about why we acted as we did if we already anticipated this outcome.

Still, if such an outcome could be foreseen . . . in 1965, why not act sooner rather than later? Or, at least, why not recommend an urgent study of the prospects and problems of such an action and the development of a possible military plan. . . . Was it just the ultimate illustration of the incremental decision-making syndrome which seeks always to avoid or postpone difficult decisions or slice them into the smallest possible bits? Only McNamara himself can provide the true answer and, so far, has chosen to remain silent.[24]

From the standpoint of the model, however, the answer to Hannah's question is obvious. In the passage Hannah quotes, McNamara was acknowledging, by implication at least, that his model for coercive bargaining with the North Vietnamese would be a very costly approach, but that it was still outside of the assumptions of his approach to adopt traditional military means and goals such as trying to isolate the North Vietnamese military forces through logistical cutoff as a step on the way to disarming North Vietnam.

Hannah then goes on to make observations on our conduct of the war which come as close as one can come to (several of) the assumptions of the McNamara model, without making them explicit:

another attempt to accomplish something without really doing it. In a way this was the leitmotif of our whole war, in which we sought to induce Hanoi to stop its invasion without actually being forced to do so.[25]

Why did we not just draw a line against invasion, marking off the territory we would defend—and then defend it by our own military means?[26]

The curious thing is that the planners of the Department of Defense did not see the prospect of engaging Hanoi's main force in southern

> Laos as a fundamental change of strategy but only as another step of linear escalation. That was all they were capable of seeing.[27]

And on our success in Thailand, in spite of McNamara, Hannah observes in his closest language to that of the model:

> Secretary McNamara had failed to distinguish between a genuine internal insurgency, largely contained within the country of origin, and external invasion, masquerading as an insurgency. *He seemed to regard insurgency and invasion as merely quantitative benchmarks on the scale of violence.* (Emphasis added.) With this premise, escalation always seems inevitable, but such escalation exists only in the mind and eye of the beholder who then imposes it on the objective situation.[28]

The answer to Hannah's ponderings, the answer which makes coherent all the evidence, is that McNamara and the department he presided over, were operating from the model for the incremental use of force to punish the adversary while seeking to coerce him against a backdrop of the threat of continued escalation (within limits!) as a basis for direct political bargaining. (In the event it was we, and not the North Vietnamese, who were coerced by the terms of the model.) This is the fundamental reason why we *refused* to isolate the battle area to induce systemic shock in North Vietnam through bombing or naval blockade; or to define strategy in any way other than different benchmarks on a scale of escalating destruction. To have done any of this would have been to shift *from* the "economically rational" activity of trading pain or its threat for desired outcomes, *back to* the putatively obsolete military activity to close with and disarm the enemy—the course which North Vietnam followed in its final, classic military invasion of South Vientam. In fact, it is clear from its absence in official memorandums, that even to concede the conceptual distinction between escalation in the level of coercive violence and escalation in the intensity of fighting to disarm the North Vietnamese would have equated to something like heresy. Although it is difficult to convince those who are convinced that McNamara and his advisers were "hawks," in fact the model is not really concerned with engaging in *military* operations at all, and that was supposedly its cleverness as a means of controlling the military by finding some role for armed force in competition with adversaries, which still fell short of threatening "crisis stability."

Consider another attempt at a balanced and general account

of our conduct of the Vietnam war, *The Irony of Vietnam: The System Worked,* by Leslie Gelb and Richard Betts.[29] Based upon detailed examination of official memorandums in the four volumes of the "Pentagon Papers," and focusing upon domestic political considerations and constraints of the concerned presidents, the analysis of the book yield insights into the compatibility of the McNamara model with the general approach to all problems of especially the Johnson administration. The thesis of the book, in brief, is that the key to explaining U.S. conduct of the Vietnam War is a matter of the proper perspective about the *raison d'être* at work: the U.S. behaved in essence as a large corporation whose *overriding* goal is simply perpetuation and stabilization of its own internal system, ad infinitum. Hence, the system of incremental pressures (short of anything decisive) to induce bargaining may not have worked in Vietnam, but it worked in Washington to deter opponents, domestic or foreign, whose logic and momentum might have replaced that system with another less stable and riskier *raison d'être*, for instance, winning wars, defeating communism, and so on.

Consider in that context the following assorted observations from *The Irony of Vietnam:*

> The result was a hodgepodge that could not work in Vietnam but did work in Washington.[30]

> The presidents and most of their senior advisers created the stakes against losing as well as the constrains against doing what was necessary to win, and accepted them.[31]

> Several of the key constraints cut both ways—that is, they were not only reasons against doing what was necessary to win but reasons incurring increased risks of losing. . . . The Great Society constraint was also a double-edged sword. . . .[32]

> Winning strategies always had to have tunnel vision, dismissing the costs and dangers they would entail. Presidents could not afford that kind of partiality. Sensitivity to trade-offs made the middle road the inevitable course for leaders with final authority.[33]

At its most general level, the Gelb-Betts thesis may simply come down to the proposition that domestic political methods and considerations drove the foreign policy of a large, commercial democracy in a faraway, limited war—which is not a very surprising thesis. More interesting is their detailed account of the "cost-effectiveness" approach to the use of armed force by civilian leadership, and to the use of chains of hypothetical constraints which *could* arise in the face of any decisive action on our part.[34] The McNamara model is the intermediate step in the analysis between the way we actually operated in Vietnam, and an account of the characteristics of a large corporatelike bureaucracy striving for stability through manipulation of gains and risks "at the margins," and led by a president doing the same toward his domestic constituents. The McNamara model explains more tightly the endless lists of hypothetical escalation scenarios intended to deter both our own and enemy military forces. Its explanatory power can be seen in another analysis which explicitly recognizes its influence in the bombing campaign of North Vietnam, the aspect of military operations over which civilian leadership had the most direct control.

Wallace J. Thies, in his detailed study of the "Rolling Thunder" bombing campaign of North Vietnam in 1965,[35] traces the intellectual origins of the Kennedy-Johnson approach to the use of force back to the ideas of William Kaufmann, Bernard Brodie, and Robert Osgood, as refined by Herman Kahn and, especially, Tom Schelling. He notes the centrality in the Johnson administration strategy of Schelling's argument that the threat of force to inflict pain be used as a bargaining tool to deter *and compel* the behavior of adversaries, quoting Schelling explicitly on this point.

> The hurting does no good directly, it can only work indirectly. Coercion depends more on the threat of what is yet to come than on damage already done. . . . The object is to exact good behavior or to oblige discontinuance of further mischief. . . .[36]

Thies then characterizes the assumptions of the Johnson administration strategy for gradually coercing North Vietnam rather than destroying its strategic resources and closing its ports.[37]

1. That a program of gradually rising military pressures would induce the government in Hanoi to end its support for the insurgency in South Vietnam.
2. That the leadership would be able to "fine tune" the Administration's actions so as to . . . "orchestrate" words and deeds. . . .
3. That the use of force would be controllable, that is, that the pressures against the North could be turned off, up or down at will.[38]

Drawing, then, upon the insights of Hannah, Gelb and Betts, and Thies (among others), it would seem that a full explanation of why we did what we did must include the following observations. While President Johnson may have leaned toward splitting the difference between the Great Society and the war effort; while there may always be a bureaucratic predeliction toward "incrementalism" and "compartmentalization" of policy; and while the American political system may generally hold to short-run domestic stability as its first priority, still, the content or substance on which all these tendencies operated during the war, was the McNamara model and its policies for the punitive use of force to induce bargaining over political and diplomatic conflicts and gains. It set the horizons within which we moved by supporting all existing tendencies for limiting the decisive use of force (e.g., the Harriman accords on Laos and LBJ's desire not to mobilize the reserves), and it provides the most direct and satisfactory explanation of *both* our refusal to adopt the traditional means of even attrition warfare—to induce shock and systemic disorder in the enemy—*and* the ease with which we allowed ourselves to be drawn into the conflict, since in theory we could stop at any "graduated" point on the "spectrum of conflict."

Domestic and Military Problems With the Model During the Vietnam War

Reflection on, and analysis of, the Cuban missile crisis and the Vietnam War suggest several problems with the McNamara model, especially when employed by a political system with a popularly elected government strongly influenced by public opinion and mass media coverage. It is important to sort out these problems, as well as the arguments for the use of the model, before proceeding to the subject of its current influence. Take first the issue of popular and press reaction to policies produced by the model's adoption. We know now with hindsight that incremental and restrained escalation of "pain infliction" on North Vietnam resulted in incremental and less than restrained U.S. domestic opposition to the war, but this outcome was predicted with uncanny prescience by the one member of the Kennedy-Johnson administration who, we saw, had refused to operate from the McNamara model during the Cuban missile crisis—CIA Director John A. McCone. In a remarkable memorandum (now declassified) sent to McNamara, McGeorge Bundy and others (including LBJ) in April 1965, McCone made the following predictions:

> We must look with care to our position under a program of slowly ascending tempo of air strikes. *With the passage of each day and each week, we can expect increasing pressure to stop the bombing. This will come from various elements of the American public, from the press, United Nations, and world opinion.* (Emphasis added.) Therefore, time will run against us in this operation and I think the North Vietnamese are counting on this.[39]

However, arguments such as McCone's seem to have made little impression on LBJ, McNamara, or other top advisers,[40] and a few months later the administrative began the escalation of troop and bombing levels. But of interest here is the issue of the prediction's accuracy, especially with regard to domestic public reaction. As a general trend, and with occasional exceptions, McCone's prediction was borne out, both with regard to the bombing and to U.S. involvement in Vietnam, with gradual drops in support of the bombing of the North and of the concomitant decision to increase troop levels. Gelb and Betts cite opinion polls showing the gradual rise from 24 percent of those interviewed in August 1965, to 46 percent in October 1967, who felt that "the U.S. had made a mistake sending troops to fight in Vietnam."[41]

Still, as is now well-established, it was the reporting of the "Tet offensive" of 1968 as a defeat for the United States and South Vietnamese which became the watershed in the flow of public opinion away from the war effort. Yet, as Gelb and Betts observe, the "centrist establishment press" had already shifted between early 1966 (*New York Times*) and Summer 1967 (*Washington Post*) away from any further escalation of the war, and toward policies of negotiation and gradual withdrawal.[42] The "Tet offensive" reporting (which never caught up in the public mind with its real military consequences as a devastating defeat for the Viet Cong[43]) was simply the event which eliminated what was left of an ambiguous middle ground in public opinion, and began to divide the electorate and the Congress into "hawks" and "doves." "Tet" was the dramatic moment when it appeared to be clear that incremental escalation was going to be too long and painful a process for *our* side.[44] On balance, McCone's prediction about the public reaction to a policy of incrementally increased "pain infliction" seems to have been borne out, and also seems in accord with commonsense observations about this democracy—its strengths are in the direction of the delights of domestic policy and the freedom it makes possible, not in the direction of any sort of complicated or sophisticated foreign and military policy, especially one repugnantly attempting to trade incremental destruction for incremental diplomatic gains, under the daily scrutiny of the mass media.

Another problem with the McNamara model for the punitive use of force is its lack of military effectiveness. I believe it is possible to identify some unambiguous military problems with the model as a basis for the use of armed force, without going into the more controversial and speculative discussion about what other approaches might have attained our aims in the Vietnam War. That is, my limited aim here is simply to point out that the McNamara model was a bad approach to the problem facing us in South Vietnam—an internal guerrilla war backed up, supplied, and manipulated by an external sovereign government and its revolutionary army, itself supplied by the Soviet Union and other Allies.

Constructive criticism of our strategy in the war falls generally into one of two camps—either (1) we should have *initially* used force to isolate and exhaust the North Vietnamese, for instance, naval blockade, bombing petroleum supplies and installations, cutting off the Ho Chi Minh trail in Laos and Cambodia;[45] or (2) that we should have combined low-level counterinsurgency warfare with efforts to help the South Vietnamese build durable political institutions.[46] These approaches do not seem to be at odds with one another—-on the contrary, both appear as necessary and complementary even from the standpoint of political and budgetary constraints, given the casualties we suffered and the dollars we eventually spent on the war, not to mention the political fallout from our failure to support the South Vietnamese. However, both propositions, in contrast to the McNamara model, clarify how force would be used. In the former case, its use is to *make* the enemy do something (that is, physically limit his capabilities) whether through battlefield defeat, or national exhaustion by way of shock and attrition, or both.[47] In the case of counterinsurgency, it is, in fact, to engage in the business of trading increments of pain for political gains, for instance, countering by quasi-military tactics a campaign of terror against civilian populations while nourishing the conditions for growth of durable political institutions. But unlike the McNamara model, these two widely divergent approaches (like those of Oriental strategists from Sun Tzu to Mao Tse Tung) both recognize a *qualitative* difference between the disarming and punitive uses of force, which has overall practical effects on outcomes by providing a standard other than the "level of destruction" for ordering military operations.

As I understand it, both the weaknesses and putative strengths of the McNamara model derive from its suppositional universality—that it is applicable for any problem in the "spectrum of conflict" from counterterrorism to nuclear deterrence. Furthermore, its proponents might add, it is agreeable to, and flows out of, American liberal traditions of concentrating on *means* rather than ends. Means are more susceptible to quantification and "cost-effective" evaluations than qualitatively different political and military ends, and might realistically provide for a long-range technique (amenable to the American commercial way) for dealing with global Leninist competition, while avoiding escalation into nuclear conflict. Furthermore, some of its defenders might even go so far as to suggest that inculcation of habits and skills of *only* punitive force is a first step in the long-range mutation of military forces into constabulary or police forces.[48] Yet, while holding off until later on such questions, and leaving aside the model's effects in the Cuban missile crisis, it is clear that its application in the Vietnam War had deleterious military and domestic consequences, and cannot be said to have "worked" at any level, except perhaps that of an autonomous Washington "logic" which severely limited the options open to one president, later driven from office, and led his predecessor not to run for another term of office.

In summary, and holding to our level of abstraction in this analysis, the Vietnam War as a whole showed that a model which views all threat and use of force on a quantitative spectrum of deterrent and coercive violence, was not "adaptive" when used by an open democratic political system as a basis for a faraway "small" war against an authoritarian political system externally supported and operating from a strategy capable of the *qualitative* leap from the police use to the decisive military use of force, short of nuclear war. If tentative agreement can be reached that general mutation of military skills (to disarm adversaries) into coercive, police, or punitive skills (to induce bargaining) may have drawbacks (1) for any system militarily; and (2) for democratic political systems domestically through adverse public reaction to sheer, incremental destruction, then it becomes important to raise the question of the model's current influence.

A final problem with the McNamara model, again probably seen as a strength by its formulators, is the way in which it allowed us to ease into armed hostilities requiring general conscription, without declaring war. Bargaining over increments of pain and the threat of their escalation, permits civilian crisis managers to maintain control over the conduct of military operations (while "keeping their options open"), as well as over the uniformed military themselves, by avoiding decisive action that would institutionally or legally imply a qualitative change in the activity pursued. This approach is consistent with the model's outlook of "deterrence and compellence" along a quantitative spectrum of pain or destruction; can be managed by those trained in economics, law, or game theory; and is primarily oriented toward coercive acts of violence while avoiding escalation into nuclear conflict, for instance, is prepared to take its bearings at all times (even in low-intensity conflict) from the dangers of accidental escalation into nuclear war, regardless of its likelihood at any moment in actual fact. And one price it pays is the willingness to see lost the strict distinction between conditions of war and peace, and with it tactical skills which arose historically in conflicts between relatively equal sovereign political entities, and which are arguably a necessary component of general deterrence in the nuclear age.

The McNamara Model's Current Influence

It is a commonplace in American government that there is little historical continuity in foreign policy, and that high political appointees are rarely familiar with what their predecessors have done. A dramatic illustration of this practical Cartesianism is to be found in the fact that there is nowhere in the State Department a record of communications between presidents of the United States and first secretaries of the Soviet Union—such documents are in the individual presidential libraries.[49] Hence, except where a treaty or pertinent law is in force, there is little likelihood that administrations will make careful considerations of the foreign and defense policies of their predecessors. In addition, as is well-known within any administration, issues tend to be fought out like legal battles in courtrooms, decided by whoever can marshall the most persuasive evidence on the day of the decision, not on the explicit basis of continuity or consistency of policy, pro or con. Furthermore, even where one can find (remarkable) consistency in a general approach as in the 1962 ExComm minutes examined earlier, it was necessary to "tease out" presuppositions implicit in what McNamara was arguing from his explicit statements. And, for the Reagan administration, we have no record comparable to the ExComm minutes of 27 October 1962.

Still, I believe it is possible to obtain from the public record a general picture of which of the McNamara presuppositions are still exerting influence, and how they are doing it. I propose in this context to look at current military doctrine and outlook; at the use of armed force in Beirut, Grenada, and Libya; at press reaction to these incidents; and at the Reagan administration's approach to arms control and deterrence.

Military Doctrine and Outlook

By way of a point of departure for this question, we might expect to find institutional memory and awareness of the McNamara model among the uniformed military themselves. And this turns out to be the case, whether in support of, or in reaction against, the McNamara outlook. Yet, it is where the influence is essentially unconscious or unperceived by the military, that it is at its greatest.

The most significant obfuscatory inheritance (with practical consequences) from the McNamara model to use all force punitively as a bargaining tool is the idea that the fundamental mission or purpose of military forces is to deter war itself. The first sentence, for example, in the 1982 version of the basic U.S. Army operations manual is the following: "THE FUNDAMENTAL MISSION OF THE UNITED STATES ARMY IS TO DETER WAR."[50] If that were in fact the case, it is difficult to see a logical argument that the military could adduce to resist its mutation into any kind of force which the secretary of defense perceived necessary as the basis for deterrence of war, including its mutation into a constabulary or police force. (In fact, as Napoleon is said by Clausewitz to have observed, the invader is always a peace-lover—he would prefer to take what he wants without resistance;[51] under such circumstances, the army might best *deter war* by simply throwing down its arms.) Surely, it is more accurate to state that the fundamental mission of the army and all U.S. forces is to stand always ready to insure the common defense and so lend support to deterrence by providing a remedy in reserve should that deterrent policy fail. The army mission statement is also remarkable in placing deterrence of war above deterrence of aggression. Both logically and practically, these two aims can pull in opposite directions. It is often the increasing threat of war which deters aggressive demands and actions, whereas satisfaction of the latter may only deter war by eliminating its requirement as a means to achieving political goals. Objectively, this can become a form of appeasement. (In the case of conflicting political demands, it can be said that peace itself—mutual deterrence—rests upon the dangers of a war which neither side wants, either because victory is improbable or because its probable costs are unacceptable.)

Now, the statement that the fundamental or "overriding mission of U.S. forces is to deter war" does make sense from the standpoint of the McNamara model, since the fundamental activity occurring under it is the use of punitive threats and reprisals to coerce desired behavior short of actual war (which would grant the uniformed military much greater influence over policy—can it be that this is the real reason we no longer declare war?) And, as a logical matter, under the McNamara model the armed forces are simply systems for the infliction of greater or lesser quantities of destruction against the hypothetical backdrop of spiraling escalation, and, hence, their fundamental mission under it really is to deter war through their sustained capability to retaliate, not contribute to deterrence of local aggression through the ability to ward off, close with, and disarm enemy forces.

To appreciate more fully the implications of this thought, contrast it with the statement that the fundamental purpose of the civil police is to deter crime or criminal behavior. Who could quarrel with this statement, since the civil police are explicitly engaged in the business of general deterrence before the fact through provision for surety and severity of punitive reprisal against the relatively few offenders who are not deterred from criminal acts by the effective domestic police monopoly of the means of physical force. (That is, the majority of potential criminal offenders are deterred not by the thought that the police can defend themselves and the populace generally, but by their overwhelming ability to disarm the offender and provide the possibility for measured retribution, a point evident in the logic of the remarks by Grotius cited at the beginning of this monograph.) Anytime that civil police begin to come up against relatively equal force, and are forced to use quasi-military tactics, we recognize this qualitative change by calling the general situations an insurrection, or even "civil war."

Yet, this is the full logical implication of the McNamara model—that if all use of force is now *qualitatively* the same regardless of the quantities of destruction involved—then the military forces are simply a very large constabulary force engaged in general deterrence of internationally "criminal" behavior. And logical implications carried in bureaucratic directives which endure over time, produce practical consequences (i.e., "theory + authority + time = practice").

The McNamara outlook on armed force can be seen most explicitly during the period of McNamara's tenure as secretary of defense. For example, the annex (on evolution of basic doctrine) to the current U.S. Air Force basic doctrine manual (AFM1–1) describes doctrinal changes introduced in 1964 in this way:

> The basic doctrine manual produced that year . . . introduced the policy of flexible response. Flexible response posited the possibility of a spectrum of conflict against which national leaders would select the best use of strategic and tactical forces to deter or decide the conflict. . . . The 1964 manual suggested that nuclear strength could deter lower level conflicts. In that context, the Air Force's primary purpose was still to deter aggression. . . .
>
> The 1964 revision . . . was the first Air Force manual of basic doctrine to omit the Principles of War.[52]

The annex then goes on to note that the 1971 revisions preserved deterrence as the "keystone of the U.S. military policy," but reflected the lessons of Vietnam and the Middle East War of 1967 in the statement that "strategic force sufficiency may not be credible deterrent against hostile acts by small powers alone," and in the recognition of the additional need of general purpose forces for deterrence.[53] And, U.S. Army basic doctrine in FM 100–5 began to include detailed accounts of the basic principles of war in 1982, following their downplay in the 1976 version, which emphasized "targeting" with fast, accurate new weapons.[54]

Yet, even as the military have come to insist on the doctrinal retention of the basic principles to ward off, close with, and disarm enemy forces, they have combined them with the general outlook of the McNamara model and its academic progenitors like Brodie, Kaufmann, Kahn, and Schelling. Take, as a salient example, the Navy's 1986 "white paper," "The Maritime Strategy,"[55] which explains the intended possible uses for former secretary John Lehman's "600–Ship Navy," and which even a sympathetic commentator described as "a discrete set of war-fighting concepts" with concepts of deterrence added.[56] The initial section on the "maritime strategy" itself, authored by Adm. James Watkins, introduces the strategy in the context of the McNamara perspective of a "spectrum of conflict." "Seapower is relevant across the spectrum of conflict from routine operations in peacetime to the provision of the most survivable component of our forces for deterring strategic nuclear war."[57] The exposition even represents the spectrum of conflict spatially on two axes labeled "Probability of Occurrence," and "Level of Violence," respectively, and showing a curve running through increasing levels of escalation from "Show of Force," to "Limited War" to "Global Conventional War," and so on.

What is most telling about this exposition is its implicit acceptance (in the use of a curve of escalating levels of *violence*) of the McNamara-Schelling assertion that what is fundamental about all use of force is the *quantity* of destruction or violence involved. (The military do not even seem to insist on the logical distinction between the purposive use of *force* and random *violence*, at nonnuclear levels.) Their general outlook, as evidenced in their various publications, is still that of the McNamara model during the Vietnam War, that the most relevant or useful fact about *any* use of force is neither its "how" nor its "why," but the amount of destruction it inflicts, or threatens to inflict in the future. Thus, for example, when the Navy authors of the "maritime strategy," go on to try to show that conventional naval war-fighting capabilities actually enhance the deterrence of war, their argumentation appears vague and intuitive, since they have moved outside of their initial assumptions about the "spectrum of conflict"—that only the threat of increasing levels of violence deters, not the now "subjective" capability to *make* enemy forces do something or not do something, that is not the traditional threat of limiting or destroying the enemy's capability to conduct operations in the relevant theater or medium (land, sea, air, or space). It would seem that if the military wish to liberate themselves from the McNamara yoke and its attendant ills (and not all do wish to), they must move outside of its economic, that is, bargaining, vocabulary, and insist (in their discussions of at least nonnuclear conflict) on the distinction between escalation in the level of destruction ("violence"), and escalation in the intensity of fighting to contain and disarm enemy forces, since the two may or may not coincide. For example, by not using force initially in a more decisive manner to disarm the North Vietnamese, that is, in a manner calculated to limit or destroy their capability to conduct operations in the South, we eventually reached a position under the Nixon presidency in which we had to use force very violently simply to gain the "slack" for an orderly withdrawal.

The Use of Force in Beirut, Grenada, and Libya

BEIRUT

From a distance, it might appear that the way Marines were used in Lebanon (and especially around the Beirut airport) would provide a classic illustration of the McNamara model in action. For example, the Marines in Lebanon were "micromanaged" from the top; placed in a militarily indefensible position under the strictest rules of engagement; and denied latitude for preemptive action to limit their own casualties.[58] When casualties began to mount to military levels following the truck bombing of the barracks at the Beirut airport, we had no choice, but to (slowly) withdraw our forces. Certainly, all that occurred was consistent with the McNamara model, but there are important differences involved.

Basically, U.S. Marines were explicitly assigned a police function or role of providing a "presence" to preserve order until foreign forces could be withdrawn from Lebanon and the Lebanese militia strengthened. Regardless of the prudence of this policy—and it might be argued that it prevented major war between Israel and Syria—there literally was no military mission involved to become confused about. U.S. forces were involved in peace-keeping and some punitive retaliatory measures such as (inaccurate) naval shelling of Druse militia positions, but were not assigned a mission which involved anything other than the threat and/or infliction of punitive reprisals (albeit from a position of insufficient overall superiority to deter). This was undoubtedly why Secretary of Defense Casper Weinberger (speaking for those in the military who think American forces were misused in Vietnam) consistently opposed the introduction of the Marines into Lebanon, or any use of military for police purposes where there was danger to life.[59]

The point here is that the *civilian* leadership in the Department of Defense stayed clear on the differences between the military and police uses of force, and the requirement for massive military superiority and the demonstrable resolve to use it decisively, if the use of military force in reprisals is to be relied upon as an effective deterrent in police actions. It was the State Department under Secretary George Schultz, assigned the responsibility for counterterrorism, which supported the introduction of Marines into Lebanon, and, in general, was more willing throughout the Reagan administration to see military force used incrementally and in punitive reprisal (and/or preemption). But for the State Department to take this position is not direct evidence of the outlook of the McNamara model, since it is the business of the State Department to further negotiations, whether by carrot or stick. In addition, the entire administration, that is, State, Defense, and the NSC, were especially concerned about accomplishing their political and diplomatic goals in Lebanon, without triggering the War Powers Resolution of 1973 by conveying the impression that U.S. forces were in a situation describable by the phrase "imminent involvement in hostilities."

It is in the provisions of the 1973 War Powers Resolution that one sees the long-range or institutional influence of the McNamara model for the punitive use of force incrementally. Passed in reaction to the unspoken "violation" of the model by the Nixon administration's intensified bombing of Laos and Cambodia (even to effect our orderly withdrawal), the resolution places the use of force over sixty days under direct legislative, and hence popular "veto." At first glance, it might appear that the intent of the 1973 resolution was to prevent precisely the use of something like the McNamara model again. But close inspection will show that this is not the case. As I understand the entire model (developed to enhance deterrence along a comprehensive spectrum of conflict), it includes the possibility of "deterring" any elements, *domestic or foreign*, viewed as potentially "destabilizing" in a crisis.[60] As we saw in the ExComm minutes of 27 October 1962, McNamara certainly used the image of escalation into nuclear war to "deter" those on the committee arguing for direct action toward Cuba. And one of the putative advantages of the model in the Vietnam war was to permit the calculated threat and use of force for political gains short of war—mobilizing the nation, calling up reserves, and so on. The point is that the overriding aim of the model, in all conflict down to counterterrorism involving the Soviet Union or its allies, is to stabilize the crisis and deter decisive escalation in the degree of "violence" by calling up in the minds of all concerned, foreign and domestic, the prospect of greater violence and destruction,[61] and heightened perceptions of the dangers of nuclear war.

In this light, the War Powers Resolution of 1973 can be seen as a "better of the worse outcomes" as conceptualized in the economic/bargaining approach to the coercive use of force in the McNamara-Schelling model. For adherents to this model, better to have attained our political aims in Southeast Asia through the incremental threat and use of force, but still desirable to habituate an electoral majority of our own population to the view that force can no longer be used except punitively. And, arguably, that has occurred through the widespread misperception that force was used decisively and massively in the Vietnam War without success. This misperception, in combination with the 1973 resolution, achieves the aim of the McNamara model to "stabilize" at least our own population in incipient crises.

LIBYA

The 15 April 1986 U.S. air raid on Libya also has dissimilarities from the McNamara model, even though the language emanating from the White House to describe our aims with regard to Colonel Qaddafi was reminiscent of the model. "The basic objective . . . is to impose enough costs in various ways, to force him to change his behavior."[62] But here, as in the case of the Beirut incident, force was being used in punitive retaliation, and (unlike the Beirut case) within the framework of overwhelming U.S. operational superiority, after the fact of terrorist attacks, both to punish and call up the specter of more punishment. And, again it was Weinberger, speaking for the Department of Defense, who opposed the use of force in this way, and the Department of State under Schultz which supported the retaliation as a form of preemptive counterterrorism (apparently permitted under National Security Decision Directive 138). Thus, there was no logical confusion over the nature of the mission which was clearly punitive and deterrent. Furthermore, the raid was conducted surreptitiously against military targets, so that it could even be argued that the punitive aspect was also militarily defensive as well, since it destroyed military assets necessary for a military response (albeit unlikely). A more accurate description, then, of the Libya raid, would be that it was a case of punitive retaliation for various wrongs received, and intended to deter future wrongs, which resembled the McNamara model in its use of military forces for punitive purposes to influence future behavior of an adversary, but which differed from the model in the use of surprise and shock, and in the intent to shift to *other* measures if this were not immediately successful, partially in anticipation of adverse public reaction to continuing strikes.[63]

GRENADA

The U.S. (and Organization of Eastern Caribbean States) invasion of Grenada on 25 October 1984 to rescue American students during a violent coup d'état (and to prevent the establishment of another Soviet satellite in the Caribbean[64]) shows little similarity to anything in the McNamara model. Although there were problems in execution and interservice coordination,[65] the use of force was not primarily punitive to induce bargaining, but was intended to disarm opposing forces, that is, close with and disarm them, and control both land and people. U.S. tactics over the six days of fighting were typical of those of the Vietnam War—that is, using fire to fix enemy positions until air strikes could "neutralize" them—but this would appear to be a tendency of a rich commercial democracy with abundant air assets. This is clearly a trend which proceeded the McNamara model, and cannot be directly attributed to it, although it certainly reinforced this trend during the Vietnam War by precluding operationally decisive ground action calculated to counter North Vietnam's capacity to support and conduct operations in the South.[66]

The point here is that while we may have been using a larger component of firepower (and hence destruction) than maneuver to achieve our military ends in Grenada, our primary aim was still tactically to dominate the enemy, not to induce bargaining through the punitive use of firepower. And, in this case, where military forces were to be used Secretary of Defense Weinberger was finally brought on board, apparently through the assurance that the military would be left in charge of operational aspects of the invasion. This is significant as another difference from the McNamara model, since detailed control of the military during the Vietnam War was justified on the grounds that the subject-matter involved was no longer strategy and tactics (now suppositionally obsolete) but bargaining through the punitive use of force, not an area of military expertise.

The McNamara Model, the Mass Media, and Public Opinion

In the April 1965 memorandum to LBJ's top defense advisers quoted earlier, CIA Director John McCone predicted that incremental increases in the bombing tempo of North Vietnam would lead to incrementally increasing domestic, press, and world opinion to stop the destruction. Not only was the prediction borne out, but it identifies a fundamental problem in the use of the McNamara model by an open democracy such as our own with daily visual and print coverage of hostilities: the daily infliction of pain, without visual indications of success, seems senseless and unpalatable to viewers, some of whom come quickly to identify their own forces as the sole source of the problem at hand, since it is they who are associated with the scenes of death and destruction. The latter is an unavoidable factor in an era of low-intensity conflict and struggle.

Consider in this context the following *Washington Post* story on the Israeli Army during the fourth month of the Palestinian uprisings in the West Bank and Gaza Strip, with the numbers of beaten and wounded in the thousands, and deaths in the scores. The story was entitled, "Israeli Army Faces Growing Criticism . . . Failure to Stop Violence Seen Underlying Attacks," and included the following statements:

> Indications that the Army's senior staff is unhappy with the policing mission it has been assigned in the territory. . . .
>
> Underlying attacks is *growing dissatisfaction with the Army's failure to stop the violence.* (Emphasis added.)
>
> "People expect the Army to be winners and instead they look like losers," said . . . editor . . . of . . . an influential newsweekly. . . .[67]

Now, the Israelis are not operating from the McNamara model; they are simply in the dilemma of trying to use military forces in police actions to deal with sustained civil resistance and violence under the scrutiny of television cameras and an attentive electorate. But the problem with the McNamara-Schelling model (which affects the Israeli government and other allies insofar as they are dependent on the American electorate for support), is that its public acceptance *exacerbates* this fundamental dilemma facing open democracies attempting to use armed force to maintain or reestablish the public order. The model first reinterprets military history to imply that all warfare has always been about trading pain for political gains,[68] and then counsels us to do this explicitly (i.e., conform our military policies and practices to its provisions), but without any attention paid to whether the American democracy (and its Allies) can function politically in this way. (Recall McGeorge Bundy's comment that he could recall no discussion of McCone's prediction about likely press reaction to incrementally increased pressures.[69])

By contrast, the *Federalist* defenders of the Constitution of 1787, at least, thought that it was *only* the ability to defend, that is, constrain and ward off adversaries *before* they could inflict devastating damage, which could move the majority of moderate citizens to take up arms, or support armed conflict for a sustained time.[70] Yet the McNamara-Schelling model simply ignored this aspect of the American political system. It took its bearings exclusively from hypotheses about nuclear war where defense before the act of destruction was indeed problematic, extending these conclusions down a suppositionally homogeneous spectrum of conflict to guerrilla warfare and insurgency, finally to assert that all use of force must now be punitively administered as part of a process of coercive bargaining and crisis management. In brief, the model never seriously considered whether it could be effective militarily at lower levels of conflict, nor what would be the likely press and public opinion reaction to incremental punitive reprisals against a backdrop of rising casualties and tactical stagnation. (The model's overriding aim, as I have tried to show, is to deter all potential disrupters, foreign and domestic, of short-term crisis stability.)

Media and Public Reaction to the Use of Force in Beirut, Grenada, and Libya

GRENADA AND LIBYA

In both of these incidents, armed force was used quickly—over a period of six days in the one case and a single morning in the other—and with surprise before press coverage could really begin to generate public opposition to the operations. Although there was predictable reaction against the Libya raid by Arab, West European, and liberal congressional and press leaders, the incident endured as a major press story for only about two days.[71] In the case of the Grenada invasion, the press were left uninformed until after the operation had begun, and only permitted to cover the story from the island, in very limited numbers, starting on the third day. There was some predictable protest against the invasion, but in combination with its (relative) military success and praise of rescued American medical students, it also was of short duration.

The real protest, which began slowly and grew in momentum over the weeks,[72] was over the decision to exclude the press from covering the operation, nominally to protect the identities of Special Operations forces. Following an initial period of support for the administration's position (NBC was apparently receiving communications ten to one in favor[73]), press, public and congressional protest eventually resulted a month later in a Joint Chiefs of Staff decision to convene a commission to study the incident and make recommendations. It was the convening of this commission in February 1984, its recommendations, and the comments of its chairman (a retired army major general), which are the important lessons for the general subject of press coverage of hostilities.

Comprised of public affairs specialists from the Department of Defense and various schools of journalism, and hearing testimony from major news organizations, the formal finding of the commission included the following statement of principle: "that the U.S. media should cover U.S. military operations to the maximum degree possible consistent with mission security and the safety of U.S. forces."[74] Although the statement would require interpretation in an actual case, the phrase about "maximum degree possible"; subsequent phrases about the imperative of "a free flow of information to the American public"; and the advice of Chairman Winant Sidle to the military to learn to "tell its story to the public," all congeal into a recommendation opposing any sustained exclusion of media coverage of hostilities involving American forces. The congressional and public support for the commission's inquiry, and the involvement of the JCS in its formation, suggest that political conditions will make it impossible to exclude press coverage of hostilities for any period longer than it takes for the press to become aware of it, in spite of various editorial calls here and there for its exclusion from battlefield hostilities.

BEIRUT

It is in the case of extended television coverage of hostilities in Lebanon, going back to the summer of 1982 and the Israeli shelling and bombing of PLO positions in West Beirut, that we can observe in incipient form, developments characteristic of McCone's 1965 predictions about public reaction to the incremental bombing of North Vietnam. As news media from across the globe began to cover the destruction in Beirut, the administration came under steady pressure from different quarters, foreign and domestic, to stop the violence and get the Israelis out of Lebanon. It is even reported that President Reagan was strongly influenced by the impact of visual coverage of Moslem civilian wounded,[75] in his initial decision to send in U.S. Marines (our part of an multinational force) as an evacuation force for the PLO fighters and as a buffer between Israelis and Arabs. And it was apparently the horror and guilt over the killing in the Palestinian refugee camps after the Marines withdrew, which influenced the administration to reintroduce twelve hundred Marines as a peace-keeping presence in Lebanon.[76]

Then, after the destruction of the Marine barracks at the Beirut airport in October 1983, Reagan was able to scotch congressional talk of withdrawal at least momentarily, with a nationally televised speech claiming that Lebanon was vital to U.S. interests.[77] But several events over the next few months resulted in a precipitous drop in public support for remaining in Lebanon: Democratic presidential candidates began to criticize Reagan for dangerous "escalation" in Lebanon; two U.S. planes were lost in an attack over Syrian territory; the U.S. battleship *New Jersey* began to shell Syrian positions in the hills east of Beirut; and the JCS began to express concern over a war with Syria.[78]

All of this came together to create the impression of a lengthy involvement in Lebanon (with no serious hope of achieving U.S. strategic goals such as expelling Syria from Lebanon), and was followed by a marked change in public opinion on our presence in Beirut. Gallup polls show the following progression: in December 1983, 48 percent of those polled believed we should withdraw troops from Lebanon; in January 1984, this increased to 57 percent; and in February 1984, 74 percent of those polled thought that we should withdraw troops.[79] And on 15 February

1984, Reagan notified Congress of his intent to remove the Marines from Beirut within thirty days, thus making explicit, a pattern implicit since the passage of the War Powers Resolution of 1973: that a voting majority of the Amerian public and its elected representatives will support U.S. military involvement in televised, international police actions only so long as casualties are very intermittent, and neither the threat of prolonged struggle, nor rapid escalation, appears imminent.[80]

The Model and Recent Arms Control/Nuclear Deterrence Policies

The model we have been critically analyzing was developed out of attempts to understand how mutual superpower possession of nuclear weapons had changed warfare (and its relation to national sovereignty). We have seen that starting from the presupposition that it was impossible to defend effectively against atomic and nuclear weapons, the conclusion was reached that armed force *at all levels* must henceforth be used only as a punitive threat to deter and compel opponents. In this context, the process of arms control became a matter of achieving stabilizing weapons and force configurations through the credible threat of mutual devastation by way of massive, posthumous (?), punitive retaliation. Stability, in turn, came to mean, following Paul Nitze among others, an assured or credible second-strike retaliatory capability.[81] International superpower competition became a matter, on this view, of maneuvering for marginal gains under the nuclear umbrella. And crisis management claimed to have replaced strategy as the comprehensive activity directing the threat and use of force.[82]

The Reagan administration appeared to challenge this general outlook with the president's 1983 speech on the Strategic Defense Initiative, but events of the past five years showed Reagan's willingness to see the program for defense against ballistic missile attack put in the general arms control process, perhaps unavoidably so for political reasons involving Congress and its various constituencies.[83] On the other hand, the "arms control process" under his administration (with its various conflicts among a diverse and rotating group of officials across several departments) differed qualitatively from that of any previous administration, including that of Nixon and Kissinger. Even the Reagan administration's "holdover" from the Kennedy-

McNamara days, Nitze, never saw the arms control process as an autonomous process for its own sake; has always been realistic about the Soviet Union; and explicitly believes that deterrence should be structured such that there is a serious capability for defense should it fail.[84] And on the other side of the Reagan administration's political spectrum, the "Report of the Commission on Integrated Long-Term Strategy," coauthored by Fred Iklé and Albert Wohlstetter, explicitly rejects the (McNamara) idea of deterrence through mutual vulnerability in favor of deterrence enhanced through new, accurate weapons capable of discrete attacks on counterforce or other military targets.[85]

However one may wish to characterize the Reagan administration's various positions on deterrence and arms control over an eight-year period, I have tried to avoid that issue head-on here[86] since (1) a less implausible case can probably be made for the McNamara model at the level of nuclear deterrence, and (2) a polemic[87] over this more ambiguous and speculative subject will detract from what I think is an ironclad case against the McNamara model as a basis for the conduct of conventional and low-intensity warfare by an open, democratic society with daily media coverage of hostilities.

Conclusion

The most serious practical defense I can think of for the McNamara model as a basis for the conduct of nonnuclear operations involving armed force or its threat, is one I have never seen fully and explicitly articulated. It is certainly not the model's own claim—as events in the Vietnam War made clear—that the incremental and punitive use of force is the way to stop small wars from becoming larger. The model's best defense (though not good enough) is a more long-range argument which would run something like this:

> The very success of Western international law and practice since Grotius in strictly demarcating between conditions of war and peace has become a liability in a nuclear age in which the West must struggle at low levels of intensity against revolutionaries who read Oriental strategists like Sun Tzu, and who see the contest as interminable (until a final demise), regardless of the particular form it takes at any moment. Under such conditions, which preclude decisive battle on a large scale, the McNamara model (or something like it) for the

> punitive use of force is the best hope for mobilizing our populations for long-term, low-level armed conflict which still falls short of threatening "nuclear stability."

This argument has a certain initial plausibility if taken in isolation from political considerations, that is, in isolation from considerations about the American political system and democracies in general. But such analytic "isolation" produces blindness about areas it is isolated from, especially long-range political considerations. (Is this not one of the hazards of adopting models devised by scientists and economists as the basis for geopolitical and military strategy?) In brief, the model *exacerbates* the tendency in advanced democracy, observed by theorists such as Plato and de Tocqueville,[88] to make the realm of domestic economic considerations the standard by which to judge all other activities. As this mutation occurs, criteria for judging success in all endeavors, including military operations, begin to approximate those of the economic science and outlook, especially the requirement for correlating quantifiable data. The budgetary and cost-effective procedures, for example, introduced by McNamara into the Department of Defense, required quantifiable data as a basis for resource management, and thus led to an emphasis in program evaluation upon hardware and firepower (weapons systems) criteria rather than upon "subjective" institutional (military) judgments as to the operational effectiveness of weapons and units. This led, in turn, to quantifiable measures of "military" success such as the number of bombs dropped, rounds fired, body counts, and pacification indexes with often only tangential relevance to overall political and military goals in Vietnam. Or, for a dramatic illustration of this "economic" outlook, consider Paul Warnke's comment on the North Vietnamese leadership upon his departure from the McNamara defense department: "We thought we were dealing with reasonable men," that is, economically rational men who should have done a cost-benefit analysis of the pain we were inflicting and desisted. Or, for an even more dramatic illustration of this quantifying tendency in an advanced democracy, consider the homogeneous spectrum of conflict critically analyzed in this article.

At the same time that the McNamara model exacerbates the unbalanced democratic tendency to judge or decide other activities by the requirements of domestic politics and economics, it ignores the "flip side" of this democratic concentration on economic and physical well-being, that is, its compassion in the face of physical distress. As John McCone foresaw in April 1965, incrementally increasing the tempo of destruction against North Vietnam would lead to incrementally increasing public opinion against it, because, to finish the analysis, it was abhorrent to watch on television, and went nowhere except toward spirited resistance to it on all sides, as the Israeli Army is discovering in the West Bank and Gaza Strip, and as would have occurred in the Beirut, Grenada, and Libya incidents had any of them begun to extend over time.

As for the current influence of the model, the ground covered in this analysis would suggest that the model's influence is at its strongest where its arguments were the most plausible, that is, at the level of crisis management between the superpowers and their major Allies; it is still prevalent but modified in arms control negotiations; and its influence is at its weakest now where it was always logically weakest, that is, as a basis for the conduct of conventional and low-intensity military operations (although, as we have seen, the military has yet *fully* to straighten out the logical fallacy in the idea that its fundamental mission is to deter war rather than enhance deterrence through capabilities to ward off, close with, and defeat should deterrence fail). Yet, it is at a more general political level, spanning the executive departments, the national legislature, and the press, by way of the War Powers Resolution of 1973 (which I have tried to show the model helped to generate), that the McNamara model still influences U.S. policy in a deleterious way.

The combination of (1) incrementally increased punitive threats and retaliation (as occurred in the Beirut incident); with (2) daily press and television coverage; and (3) facing the potential constraints of the War Powers Resolution, constitute a recipe for failure in the use of force for political ends, even when the end is essentially a negative one of maintaining the status quo. As George Schultz said in 1984, under these conditions, our adversaries know they can simply wait us out.[89] One hopes that this analysis of how and why the McNamara model was erroneously applied to lower levels of armed conflict is a step in the direction of rectifying a wrong-headed approach. Since change is not likely to occur in the latter two constraints for obvious political reasons after two decades of the model's domestic influence, a realistic prescription for success would seem to lie in the direction of the use of force to disarm the adversary locally (whether through logistical isolation or battlefield decision, or both[90]), if force is to be used at all. This will require among other things, that the uniformed military understand clearly the logical differences between the military operational and police (or punitive[91]) uses of force (even when they are required by political leadership to function as police forces[92]), in order to resist the unwitting mutation over time of their skills and force structure into those of a police or constabulary force,[93] albeit one with an air force and navy. And this they are obliged to do, not out of perverse resistance to the "tide of history,"[94] but because the military capabilities to ward off, close with, and disarm adversaries in nonnuclear conflict,[95] are still demonstrably adaptive skills for the maintenance of our political values, values which could probably not recognizably survive a long duration of ubiquitous, low-intensity "police actions."

1988–89

Notes

Thanks to the U.S. Institute of Peace, Washington, D.C., for their grant, and to various members of the teaching and library staff at the Naval War College, Newport, Rhode Island, and to the U.S. Air Force Academy, Colorado Springs, for assistance in obtaining information. A shorter, somewhat altered, version of this monograph appeared in *Strategic Review* 17, no. 4 (Fall 1989): 18–30. The implications of the conduct of the 1991 Gulf War for this monograph's subject are stated briefly in the introduction to this collection.

1. James Webb, "At Least the Navy Knows What it's Doing in the Gulf," *Washington Post*, 20 April 1988, A–21. For a follow-up on Webb's assertion, see n. 92.

2. An entire section of this article is devoted to a demonstration of this assertion.

3. "The exemplary formal strategist was Thomas Schelling. . . ." Lawrence Freedman, *The Evolution of Nuclear Strategy* (New York: St. Martin's Press, 1983), 181. On the influence in the McNamara defense department of Schelling's view of warfare as coercive bargaining, see Fred Kaplan, *The Wizards of Armageddon* (New York: Simon & Schuster, 1983), chap. 23, especially 332, which includes the following statements: "When in the early months of 1964, government officials laid plans to step up military action against North Vietnam, it was precisely this concept of coercive warfare that shaped the resulting strategy. This was the natural outcome not only of McNamara's own proclivity toward controlling force rationally, but also of the coincidence that one of McNamara's closest advisers on Vietnam . . . happened to be one of Tom Schelling's most dedicated devotees, a Harvard Law School professor named John McNaughton."

4. See, for example, Schelling, *Arms and Influence* (New Haven, Conn.: Yale University Press, 1966).

5. For a discussion, see my 1983 monograph, "Accidental Nuclear War and

Deterrence," in Wendell J. Coats, Jr. *The Activity of Politics and Related Essays*, (London and Toronto: Associated University Presses, 1989), 72–104.

6. For a fairly comprehensive overview of the literature, see Lawrence Freedman, *Evolution of Nuclear Strategy*, sec. 4–8, notes.

7. For the traditional view, see, for example, Clausewitz's *On War*, any edition, chap. 1. All quotes are from Schelling, *Arms and Influence*, v–34.

8. For a discussion of what such a strategy would have meant in the naval war against Vietnam, see William R. Hawkins, "Strategy and 'Freedom of Navigation,'" *The National Interest*, no. 12 (Summer 1988): especially 54–56. For a summary of Delbrueck's views, see Gordon A. Craig, "Delbrueck: The Military Historian," in *Makers of Modern Strategy*, edited by Peter Paret (Princeton, N.J.: Princeton University Pres, 1986), especially, 341–42. For the classic discussion of the theory of air power, see Guilio Douhet, *The Command of the Air* (1921. Reprint. New York: Arno Press, 1972), especially 51. "Keep in the mind the following basic principle, which is the same one which governs warfare on land and sea: *Inflict the greatest damage in the shortest possible time.*"

9. "October 27, 1962: Transcripts of the Meetings of ExComm," transcribed, McGeorge Bundy, edited by James Blight, *International Security* 12, no. 3 (Winter 1986–1988): 30–92.

10. Ibid., 52.

11. Ibid., 55.

12. Ibid., 63.

13. Ibid., 75 n. 20.

14. Ibid., 75.

15. Ibid., 78.

16. Ibid., 83–84.

17. Ibid., 88.

18. See, in this connection, Sean Wilentz's review essay of Tuchman, *The First Salute: A View of the American Revolution, The New Republic*, 29 November 1988, especially 32.

19. "U.S. Strategic Air Power, 1948–1962," eds. Richard Kohn and Joseph Harahan, *International Security* 12, no. 4 (Spring 1988): 92–93. Also interesting in this connection are observations on the crisis of former NSC adviser McGeorge Bundy. "We did not fully understand the strength of our own hand. Partly . . . this was a consequence of our exaggerated fear of the operability of the Cuban missiles. But our more serious failure was not to recognize the strength of our position—in both conventional military strength and political persuasiveness." McGeorge Bundy, *Danger and Survival* (New York: Random House, 1988), 457. See also the newspaper converage of a two-day Moscow conference on the Cuban missile crisis which reports Kruschev's son, then a rocket engineer, as saying that twenty warheads were already on Cuba, but that Soviet officers had no orders to use them even if the island were invaded. Also reported is the disclosure that the Soviets had only twenty intercontinental missiles pointed at the United States during the crisis, fifty-five fewer than the figure of seventy-five in U.S. intelligence estimates at the time. *New York Times*, 29 January 1989, A1 and A10.

20. Raymond Garthoff, "Cuban Missile Crisis: The Soviet Story," *Foreign Policy*, no. 72 (Fall 1988): 79.

21. Norman Hannah, *The Key to Failure: Laos and the Vietnam War* (Lanham, Md.: Madison Books, 1987).

22. Ibid., xvi.

23. Ibid., 223.
24. Ibid.
25. Ibid., 231.
26. Ibid., 215.
27. Ibid., 234.
28. Ibid., 219.
29. Leslie Gelb and Richard Betts, *The Irony of Vietnam: The System Worked* (Washington, D.C.: The Brookings Institution, 1979).
30. Ibid., 290.
31. Ibid., 268.
32. Ibid., 270.
33. Ibid., 271.
34. For example, consider the following: "Those who wanted to keep the risks of winning and losing in balance were always introducing new constraints to meet new pressures. To stifle the demands for winning generated in the wake of the Tet offensive in 1968 . . . the task force arrayed the following arguments. . . . 'We will have failed . . . if the war spreads to the point where . . . there is direct military confrontation with China . . . other commitments are no longer credible . . . the slogan 'No more Vietnams' brings other commitments 'into question', . . .'" Gelb and Betts, *Irony of Vietnam*, 271.
35. Wallace J. Thies, *When Governments Collide: Coercion and Diplomacy in the Vietnam Conflict, 1964–1968* (Berkeley: University of California Press, 1980).
36. Ibid., 9.
37. Again, on our refusal to employ a strategic naval blockade of North Vietnam, see the article by Hawkins cited in n. 9.
38. Thies, *When Governments Collide*, 9.
39. Memorandum for Secretary of State, Secretary of Defense, Special Assistant for NSA, Ambassador Maxwell Taylor, from Director, CIA, dated 2 April 1965, declassified from "Top Secret" on 4/19/78 and currently on file as document #75a of National Security Council History, Deployment of Major U.S. Forces to Vietnam, July 1965, 2, Box 40, LBJ Library, Austin, Texas. (A Shorter version, listed as document #74c, was sent to LBJ.)
40. "In particular, I do not have any recollection about the paragraph on likely press reaction," wrote McGeorge Bundy in response to my query about the reaction to the McCone Memorandum at the time. Private correspondence to the author, dated 9 November 1988.
41. Gelb and Betts, *Irony of Vietnam*, 218.
42. Ibid., 214–15.
43. See, in this connection, Peter Braestrup, *Big Story* (Garden City, N.Y.: Anchor Books, 1978).
44. See, in this connection, the videocassette documentary, "Television's Vietnam," copyright 1984, 1985, by Accuracy in Media, Inc.
45. For example, see Norman Hannah, *The Key to Failure* [Foreword by Col. (Ret.) Harry Summers].
46. See, for example, Andrew Krepinevich, Jr., *The Army and Vietnam* (Baltimore, Md.: Johns Hopkins University Press, 1986). Interestingly, Major Krepinevich acknowledges intellectual guidance from former McNamara consultant, William Kaufmann (p. xv).
47. It should be clear that I am suggesting that traditional attrition warfare *and* "battlefield decision" warfare have more in common than either has with

the McNamara model—that is, both intend to *make* the enemy do something rather than induce him to "change his behavior." To take an obvious example, blockade of an adversary's surface-to-air missile supplies will eventually close down his high-altitude antiaircraft capabilities, regardless of his calculations of costs, benefits, and so forth.

48. See, for example, Adam Yarmolinsky and Gregory D. Foster, *Paradoxes of Power* (Bloomington: Indiana University Press, 1983).

49. From a presentation by Richard Pipes at a conference of the Center for the Study of the Presidency, Boston, 12 November 1988.

50. FM 100–5, "Operations," Department of the Army, Washington, D.C., 1982, 1. (I am informed that the 1986 restricted version of FM 100–5 retains this statement without substantial alteration.)

51. "The aggressor is always peace-loving (as Bonaparte always claimed to be); he would prefer to take over our country unopposed. To prevent his doing so one must be willing to make war and be prepared for it." Carl von Clausewitz, *On War*, edited and translated by Michael Howard and Peter Paret (Princeton, N.J.: Princeton University Press, 1976), 370.

52. "Functions and Basic Doctrine of the United States Air Force," AFMI–1, January 1984 (n.p.), A–4.

53. Ibid., A4–A5.

54. FM 100–5, "Operations," Department of the Army, 1976. See also the characterization of the 1976 version of FM 100–5 in Boyd Sutton "Strategic and Doctrinal Implications of Deep Attack Concepts for the Defense of Central Europe," in *Military Strategy in Transition: Defense and Deterrence in the 1980s*, edited by Keith Dunn and William Staudenmaier (Boulder, Colo. Westview Press, 1984), 60–83, which includes the following statements: "FM 100–5, *Operations*, in 1976 . . . was regarded as excessively reactive, ceding the initiative to the attacker by discouraging maneuver of forces . . . it was said to focus inordinately on massing firepower. . . ."

55. "The Maritime Strategy," U.S. Naval Institute (Annapolis, Md.: January 1986).

56. F. J. West, Jr., "Maritime Strategy and Nato Deterrence," *Naval War College Review* (September–October 1985): 12.

57. Ibid., 7.

58. For an account based on interviews with military personnel present, see Richard A. Gabriel, *Military Incompetence* (New York: Hall and Wang, 1985), 117–47.

59. Secretary Weinberger's general position about not using military forces except for military missions, and not without the support of the American people, has come to be known as the "Weinberger doctrine."

60. For two recent expressions of the view that the real danger facing the world is the military in both the United States and the Soviet Union, see Kenneth Galbraith, "The Military: A Loose Cannon?" *Parameters* 17, no. 1 (Spring 1987): 94–96 (reprint, *Harper's Magazine*); and Arthur Schlesinger, Jr., "The Military and the Nuclear Arms Race," *Parameters* 17, no. 2 (Summer 1987), especially 101, which reproduces the following from President Kennedy in 1963: "'Mr. Kruschev and I occupy approximately the same political positions inside our governments. He would like to prevent a nuclear war but is under severe pressure from his hardline crowd. . . . The hardliners in the Soviet Union and the United States feed on one another.'" (Reprinted from *The Cycles of American History*.) Also interesting in this context is the discussion in Plato's

Statesman of the recurring tension *within* any political community between the "spirited" and the "moderate" over foreign policy, and the need for the statesman to balance their opposing claims rather represent one side, exclusively.

61. Again, the model never intends for escalation into higher conflict really to occur, as its various formulators made increasingly clear in their public writings over the past decades. But, from the standpoint of this article, what is of interest is that even calls for greater reliance on conventional forces as the basis for deterrence by proponents of the McNamara model, contain no discussion of traditional military uses for them—they are still intended to stretch out the time for negotiations to end incipient hostilities. See, for example, McGeorge Bundy, George Kennan, Robert McNamara, and Gerard Smith, "Nuclear Weapons and the Atlantic Alliance," *Foreign Affairs* 60, no. 4 (Spring 1982), especially 761–62.

62. R. W. Apple, Jr., "U.S. Said to Hope Clashes Prompt Moves in Libya to Oust Qaddafi," *New York Times*, 3 April 1986, A12. Other language emanating from the administration was even more characteristic of the McNamara model, with phrases about providing Qaddafi with incentives to alter his criminal behavior—in explicit reference to the April 15 raid.

63. "Peter Rodman of the NSC staff wrote a memo saying that public opinion would only stand for one more strike so it had better be a good one." David C. Marin and John Walcott, *Best Laid Plans* (New York: Harper & Row, Publishers, 1988), 315.

64. For an attempt to balance the good accomplished by the invasion against the objections of the Organization of American States (OAS) and other Allies, see Alberto R. Coll, "Why Grenada Was Important," *Naval War College Review* 40, No. 3 (Summer 1987), especially 17.

65. For an account, see Gabriel, *Military Incompetence*, 149–86.

66. Ibid., 176. General Westmoreland called this approach a "fire-base psychosis" during the Vietnam War. See David Palmer, *Summers of the Trumpet* (Novato, Calif.: Presidio Press, 1978), 107–115, 143–45.

67. Carried in *The Washington Post*, 7 March 1988, 23.

68. See Schelling, *Arms and Influence*, chap. 1.

69. In private correspondence—see n. 41.

70. See, for example, *Federalist* #23, any edition. The *Federalist* writers also thought that the criterion of the common defense would restrain aggressive military ambitions, a built-in safeguard lacking in the McNamara model, which has no *institutional* constraints on the quantity of destruction inflicted.

71. That is, 15 and 16 April 1986.

72. For an account, see "Anybody Want to Go to Granda," *Time*, 14 November 1986, 70.

73. Ibid.

74. Quoted in "The Military and the Press: Is the Breach Worth Mending?" *Army*, 35, no. 2 (February 1985), by Maj. Gen. (ret.) Winant Sidle, 24–25.

75. Reported by David K. Hall in an unpublished Naval War College case study, "Lebanon Revisited" (n.d.), 5.

76. Roy Gutman, "Battle Over Lebanon," *Foreign Service Journal*, June 1984, 28–33; reprint, Hall, "Lebanon Revisited."

77. Hall, "Lebanon Revisited," 32.

78. Ibid., 25.

79. Ibid.

80. For a realistic scenario in which this pattern occurs, see William A. Rusher, "The Media and Our Next Intervention: Scenario," *Parameters* 18, no. 3 (September 1988): 2–12.

81. For an account of the evolution of Nitze's strategic views and their influence, see Gary L. Sojka, "The Strategic Thought of Paul H. Nitze," *Naval War College Review* (March–April 1984): 52–68.

82. A view of McNamara though not of Nitze.

83. For a detailed account of this history, see Strobe Talbott, *The Master of the Game* (New York: Alfred A. Knopf, 1988).

84. Ibid., throughout.

85. "Discriminate Deterrence," Report of the Commission on Integrated Long-Term Strategy" (Washington, D.C.: U.S. Government Printing Office, 1988), 30–42.

86. I have discussed the McNamara model and nuclear deterrence, elsewhere—refer to n. 6.

87. For the view that the Reagan administration completely sold out the Strategic Defense Initiative program to the arms control process, see Malcolm Wallop and Angelo Codevilla, *The Arms Control Delusion* (San Francisco: ICS Press, 1987).

88. It does not seem persuasive to quote Plato on democracy to Americans, but see the views of an acknowledged friend of democracy on this point: de Tocqueville, *Democracy in America*, 2, 2, 10 ("Of the Taste for Physical Well-Being in America"), any edition.

89. Schultz's exact words were reported to be that the resolution "practically invites our adversary to wait us out. . . ." Speech to the Trilateral Commission, April 1984, quoted in Hall, "Lebanon Revisited," 34.

90. Such as occurred in the 1991 war with Iraq.

91. It is important to emphasize that the punitive use of force in reprisal to deter future wrongs has a long history in international practice, and differs from the McNamara-Schelling model in that it is *not* intended to induce a political settlement (e.g., compel the adversary to the negotiating table), but simply to induce the adversary to *desist* from further maltreatment of prisoners or other terrorist action. Additionally, it makes little sense to use force in this fashion unless one is prepared to resort to genuine military use of force should the adversary begin to respond in kind.

92. For example, the mission of U.S. naval forces criticized by former secretary of the navy, James Webb, in the quotation cited at the beginning of this article. That mission was explicitly a police function: the safeguarding of property against potential assailants. If there were ulterior U.S. strategic objectives beyond this police function and the broad aim of "projecting U.S. power into the Persian Gulf," for instance, the objective of preventing Iran's victory in the war with Iraq—those were never spelled out. And the issue devolved simply to the question: how much force should the "cop-on-the-beat" exercise appropriate to his mission and at the least risk to himself.

93. For a discussion of some of the problems involved in shifting troops back and forth from military to police functions, see Frank Kitson, *Low-Intensity Operations* (London: Faber, 1971).

94. For an example of what I call the "direction of history" argument, see Adam Yarmolinsky and Gregory D. Foster, *Paradoxes of Power* (Bloomington: Indiana University Press, 1983), especially 148. "Beyond the horizons of current arms control efforts lies the distant prospect of a world in which . . . the

United States military can be converted from a war-fighting to a constabulary force."

95. Here is a good place to show the connection of my phrase, "ward off, close with, defeat, and disarm," with traditional military usage. By this phrase I mean operational superiority (the capability to maneuver freely in the relevant medium) gained by tactical operations (ward off and close with) resulting in tactical victory (defeat). Military victory includes the broader aspect of controlling land and people (the enemy political base in the theater of operations). For an extended discussion of this view of the traditional military vocabulary, see Maj. Gen. (Ret.) Wendell J. Coats, Sr., "Clausewitz's Theory of War: An Alternative View," *Comparative Strategy* 5, no. 4 (1986): 351–73.

4
Drama and Democracy

> The intuitive and the speculative understanding took up hostile attitudes toward their respective fields, whose boundaries they now begin to guard with jealousy and distrust. . . .
>
> —Schiller, *Sixth Letter*

This essay takes as its point of departure, the same Aristotelian observation as the title essay about (even the best sort of) democracy—that its citizens must continually be led up from a subpolitical outlook focusing on personal happiness, family, and reputation, if the regime is to endure. The first essay isolated the role of military service in teaching the majority of citizens in popular government to think in terms of, and deliberate within, a system of authority comprised of general laws directed to the common advantage (or a common object of good). This essay first looks at the way in which a development concurrent with the rise of modern democracy—modern science—fosters a leveling outlook which may be described as unpolitical; and then tries to illustrate how intelligent drama may be used pedagogically to help remedy the "homogeneous" outlook nurtured by the predominance of scientific ways of explaining in our civilization.

Whatever their differences and ancient quarrels, political theory and classical (and some modern) drama have, vis-à-vis modern science, one very important thing is common. Both accept, explain, and remain within, the idea of ordered wholes—wholes whose unity and coherence is achieved in a synthesis or integration of both likes and unlikes. In this case, the ordered whole they both accept is that of human society or community. Both the political theorist and the (pre-"postmodern") dramatist are engaged in explaining or exploring what they perceive to be actual relationships of equality and hierarchy among types of human beings in society with one another, regardless of the ideological disposition of the moment, or whether they accept it or are critical of it. (Obviously, this observation becomes less accurate in cases of drama written for audiences already in a state of disorder—consider for example from the ancient world, the case of Euripides *Orestes.*[1])

Modern science, on the other hand, explains in a much simpler and more homogeneous fashion—generally along the lines of what we know as a mathematical function. To explain or account for something on the scientific view, is to classify it as a function or illustration of a presupposed unity of variables, for instance, a law of physics such as $V = gt$. In this way of explaining, a falling apple, for example, is first resolved into a generic abstraction called "mass," and then accounted for as an illustration of the general law for computing velocity for a falling object. Now, while this may be an intelligent way of accounting for changes in physical reality, when its method of explaining is extended into the world of human action, it can produce dubious "side effects" on the explainer. Over time, explaining human events (regardless of how successfully) as illustrations of general laws understood as relationships of variables themselves indifferent to the fortunes of human beings, can become a self-fulfilling prophecy. As succeeding generations are taught to see themselves as illustrations of scientific "laws"—for example, "my economic choices today are an illustration of the law of downward sloping demand," or "this is an excellent case of regression toward the mean"—the personalities involved become simpler and more "homogeneous" because their models, metaphors, and concepts of self-expression, self-enactment, and self-disclosure, have all become more so, as well. In brief, the spread of scientific explanation as *the* serious (and legitimate and resource deserving) mode of explanation means that the primary context for human understanding of its own actions mutates from the moral to the statistical and "lawlike."[2]

This observation is perhaps not unfamiliar, but to extend the argument, the general effect of the predominance of this scientific outlook is to encourage and nourish the tendency of democracy to view things in subpolitical terms; and to direct its citizens away from languages, concepts, and time-conceptions[3] which would facilitate their grasping higher-order political abstractions such as authority and a common object of good. This is to say that important political abstractions such as "justice," concerned about linking together in a meaningful way, diverse but recurring human activities and endeavors, can only with the greatest difficulty be grasped as real by minds constituted exclusively in the subpolitical languages of physical science, medicine, economics, experimental psychology,[4] and so on. Furthermore, given the hostility of both modern science and democracy to political theory, the chances for a widespread interest in that subject are also slim. But the pedagogical employment of drama from less reductivist ages,[5] might be a way of preserving the more complex view of human society as a mixture of likes and unlikes, and hence always requiring political explanation and orientation for the cultivation of intelligent diversity.[6]

I propose in this essay to try to support and illustrate this claim by looking at several disparate instances of drama from the standpoint of what they have to teach students (and future citizens and leaders) of the potential ills of leveling forces such as modern science in the service of modern democracy (or, increasingly—with the spread of high technology into more aspects of human life—modern democracy in the service of modern science). I shall begin by looking at the case of Dr. Stockmann in Ibsen's *Enemy of the People*, a character of scientific rather than political outlook; then at Brecht's Galileo, a character of scientific outlook who comes round to a more political one; then, on the general subject of political justice, at the characters of Creon and Antigone in Sophocles' *Antigone*, Cytemnestra, Agamemnon, and Orestes in Aeschylus' Orestian trilogy, and some characters in Camus's *Les justes;* and, finally, at the light to be shed on the limits of political justice in Shakespeare's *Tempest*.[7] And, I shall consider all of them within the general context of human society understood as a hierarchy of likes and unlikes requiring political integration in its most balanced and viable form.

An Enemy of the People

Henrik Ibsen's 1882 play, *An Enemy of the People*, concerns an incident in a small Norwegian town, which occurs when an idealistic medical doctor, Dr. Stockmann, discovers that the tannery industry is polluting the nearby spas with invisible organisms known as bacteria. As the economic consequences for the town of admitting this strange new discovery sink into the consciousness of the citizenry, the doctor loses public support and is driven into a radical stance which results in the virtual exile of himself, his family, and the new group of young disciples he will choose to reform humanity. Although Ibsen (of the "middle period") is clearly supportive of Dr. Stockmann as an agent of revolutionary change and progress,[8] it is not necessary to agree entirely with Ibsen's (or any other skillful dramatist's) own sympathies to find the play useful for our pedagogical purposes, that is, gaining insight into the structure of human communities under varying conditions.

Dr. Stockmann, our protaganist, is idealistic, intense, and competent in technical matters, but somewhat naive about people and politics. He is much like his daughter, Petra, who admires him and says, "He's wonderful, he's not giving in," after Stockmann demands the freedom to express himself on "any problem under the sun," even, "if all the world caves in."[9] Stockmann's brother, Peter, the mayor, by contrast, is authoritative, and primarily interested in the town and his position in it. He is something of a caricature in his directness, but nevertheless expresses serious positions on political realities, telling Dr. Stockmann such things as "the individual has to subordinate himself to the whole . . . or . . . those authorities charged with the common good."[10] He also tries to explain to the doctor that the problem facing the town is "a mixture of both technical and economic considerations"[11] (or, by implication, following Aristotle's definition of politics as the architectonic art, a *political* matter).

There are other general *types* depicted in Ibsen's play, as well. Stockmann's father-in-law is a shrewd businessman, unbelieving in scientific discoveries about invisible organisms in the water, who decides that Stockmann must be trying to drive down the price of stock in the baths in order to buy it all up on the cheap before recanting—and so, does just that himself, and with the funds he had intended as the inheritance for Stockmann's own sons (as insurance that Stockmann will follow through on such a course). There is even in the play a small businessman, Aslaksen, representing unreflective moderation grounded in the need for economic security. There are two journalists who initially support Dr. Stockmann's revolutionary discovery, until its economic consequences dawn upon their readers, and the journalists reverse themselves with the statement, "Any man who'd destroy a whole community must be a public enemy."[12] There is Stockmann's wife, who foresees much better than her husband, the struggle facing her family, but stands by him anyway. Finally, there is the independent ship's captain, Horvster, who supports Stockmann (as he would any independent character or thinker) with a Socratic-like observation, "At sea it wouldn't work too well" for all to steer.[13]

As events unfold and Dr. Stockmann (who has never thought about politics and alliance building at all) realizes, contrary to his expectations, that the town is not going to act upon his report, he makes a public presentation, hostilely delivered and hostilely received by his audience. In his remarks, Stockmann makes several immoderate and imprudent observations about the great majority of people.

> The most insidious enemy of the truth and freedom among us is the solid majority . . . the damned, solid, liberal majority. . . .
>
> The majority is never right. . . . This is one of those social lies that any free man who thinks for himself has to rebel against. . . I'll be damned . . . if its part of the eternal plan that the stupid are meant to rule the intelligent.
>
> There's a terrible gap between the thoroughbreds and the mongrols in humanity . . . as soon as I extend the law to the two-legged animals, Mr. Hovstad stops cold. He doesn't dare think his thoughts any longer, or follow his ideas to a logical conclusion.[14]

It is clear at this point that Dr. Stockmann has given up any chance that might have remained to get community action on his discovery about the pollution of the baths. But, more important for our purposes, is his view of his fellow citizens, all of whom are judged from what we might call a "scientific" perspective. Out of a naive idealism gone sour, Stockmann turns his reductivist, scientific method onto political and communal life to read partial truths the ultimate truth about which is that they should not be publically spoken, or not without preparation and qualification. (Obviously, Ibsen would disagree.) Ibsen's Dr. Stockmann cannot see—because he cannot focus on a community, per se—that the *partial* blindnesses of his fellow citizens are what make them capable of striving, of doing their respective jobs.

For example, without his attachment to preeminence and authority, the mayor could not do his job of leading the city; the journalists' ability to manipulate the public (up to a point) is tied to their closeness and responsiveness to the mood of that public; the small businessman's attachment to economic security is one source of continuity and stability in the community as a whole; and the ship captain's unreflective independence of character provides the support for revolutionary characters like Dr. Stockmann himself. But the point for our analysis is this:

while Ibsen was perhaps aware of all of this in spite of his apparent sympathy for "Stockmann-like" characters, could a generation raised exclusively on Stockmann's outlook—on the application of this scientific method to political life—any longer grasp the recurring connections among different *types* of people in proximity to one another in communities, much less appreciate what they make possible? (The political issue for student analysis, is whether a less extreme and more prudent Dr. Stockmann might have been able to provide the leadership necessary to clean up the public baths.)

Galileo

In this post–World War II (i.e., atomic age) treatment of Galileo's retraction before the Catholic Church by the German, Marxist playwright, Bertolt Brecht, the tension between scientific truth and political prudence is central as with Ibsen's *Enemy of the People.* (Brecht apparently wrote a prewar version of the play which had a considerably different outcome and emphasis.[15])

In Brecht's drama, we are presented with a scientist, passionate like Dr. Stockmann about the scientific truth of the physical universe, and naive about politics.

> *Galileo.* I believe in the human race. The only people who can't be reasoned with are the dead. Human beings are intelligent. . . . The evidence of your eyes is a very seductive thing. Sooner or later everybody must succumb to it.
>
> *Sagredo.* Galileo . . . you are suspicious and skeptical in science, but in politics as naive as your daughter. How can people in power leave a man at large who tells the truth. . . . Can you see the Pope scribbling a note in his diary: "Tenth of January, 1610, Heaven abolished?"[16]

But unlike (the Teutonic) Stockman, (the Latin) Galileo is also realistic about his need for money, and is something of a sensualist as well.

> *Galileo.* Your father, my dear, is going to take his share of the pleasures of life in exchange for all his hard work. . . . I have no patience . . . with a man who doesn't use his brains to fill his belly.[17]

> *Galileo.* I cherish the consolations of the flesh. I have no patience with cowards who call them weaknesses.[18]

In Brecht's drama, Galileo is confronted with the following arguments from the Church about publishing his claim that the earth revolves around the sun, rather than vice versa:

> *Cardinal Bellarmin.* Let's move with the times. If it makes navigation easier for sailors to use new charts based on a new hypothesis, let them have it. We have only to scotch doctrines that contradict Holy Writ. . . . Tonight the Holy Office has decided that the theory according to which the earth goes around the sun is foolish, absurd, and a heresy. I am charged, Mr. Galilei, with cautioning you to abandon these teachings. . . .
>
> *Galileo.* But the facts. . . .
>
> *Cardinal Bellarmin.* It is not given to man to know the truth: it is granted to him to seek after the truth. Science is the legitimate and beloved daughter of the Church.[19]

But Galileo does not abandon his teachings, and after they begin to have a deleterious effect on the faith of common people ("Galileo, the Bible-killer"), the Church finally resorts to the threat of torture, allowing Galileo to see the actual instruments that might used on him. In Brecht's play, the threat is sufficient (along with his daughter's religious faith) to convert Galileo into a more or less willing servant of the Church, and to betray his science.

> *Galileo.* I recanted because I was afraid of physical pain. . . . They showed me the instruments.
>
> *Andrea.* It was not a plan?
>
> *Galileo.* It was not.[20]

In his final speech, Galileo goes on to explain that he doubts he was ever in much danger; that he betrayed his profession by allowing the powers that be to have his discovery and release only so much as would not disturb the peace; and that science in the hands of established powers may simply be used to keep most human beings in drudgery. If I follow Brecht's implication in Galileo's long, final speech, it is that neither established powers, not scientists themselves are the best guide for the uses of scientific discovery, but rather the needs of the people at large.

> *Galileo.* In my day astronomy emerged into the market place. At that particular time, had one man put up a fight, it could have had wide repercussions.[21]

As the play ends, Galileo (somewhat indifferently) gives to his former assistant a copy of his discourse on motion which he has managed, without much sacrifice, to rewrite and conceal from Church authorities; his assistant, in turn, smuggles it out of Italy. If I follow Brecht here, the implication of the dramatic events is, again, that "the people" may not count exclusively on great scientists for relief of the human condition (and certainly not on established authorities), but must rely upon themselves for the spread and proper containment of the fruits of applied science. Here are the play's closing lines, addressed to no one in particular:

> May you now guard science' light
> Kindle it and use it right,
> Lest it be a flame to fall
> downward to consume us all.[22]

It is interesting here to contrast the views of Brecht's Galileo and Ibsen's Dr. Stockmann in the context of our theme about science and politics. Stockmann sees the people at large as ignorant and cowardly forces of reaction, requiring independent and courageous researchers and leaders to shepherd them toward radical change. Brecht's Galileo (and the play as a whole) sees the people as the guardians of scientific discovery in the service of relief of the human estate, against authorities who will use science only to preserve the established order, and keep them in drudgery; and sees scientists, who once they no longer labor in the service of "the truth of humanity," as in danger of producing something horrible.

> *Galileo.* Should they, then, in time, discover all there is to be discovered, your progress must become a progress away from the bulk of humanity. The gulf might even grow so wide that the sound of your cheering at some new achievement would be echoed by a universal howl of horror.[23]

What both the characters of Stockmann and Galileo share, however (and, by implication, their creators), is the visionary hope for a world where the recurring tensions which call forth the need for political authority and political means for their moderate reconciliation, will no longer exist. And both are also naive in their most basic assumptions: Ibsen in the belief that "courageous elites" would not produce something horrible; Brecht in the belief that the "needs" of the bulk of humanity would not issue in something repulsive (in its reductivisim) were they to set the directions of scientific inquiry.[24] Having looked at the dramatic conception of an outlook animated by the hope of "homogenizing" human society in the overriding interest of relief of the human condition, let us turn to some depictions of the idea of political justice as a way of holding in balance the "likes and unlikes" of human society.

Antigone

Much has been made of Sophocles' mid-fifth-century B.C. tragedy. Hegel, especially, was fond of employing lines and themes from *Antignone* to illustrate aspects of what he called Greek ethical consciousness, and its male and female counterparts; and Aristotle employed it (and the entire Theban trilogy) in the *Poetics* to illustrate an aspect of plot construction in tragedy. But I propose to show how it may be employed pedagogically as an antidote for the modern democratic and scientific tendency to view human society as a homogeneous aggregate rather than a coherent unity of likes and unlikes.

In this tragedy, a headstrong young woman, the product of an incestuous union, and a ferocious lover of her own family's honor, confronts her uncle, a ruler, over his edict that her brother be left unburied for leading an attack upon his own city (Thebes). The young woman, Antigone, has on her side the will of the gods that human dead be buried, although this is not the primary reason for her spirited resistance; rather, it is her intense love of her own family's honor, and a preoccupation with death and its rituals (perhaps symbolic of the hostility to regeneration of the act of incest). Antigone's uncle, King Creon, has on his own side the political necessity to preserve his city from peril by making an example of anyone who threatens its existence; but his spirited resistance to changing his edict against burial for Antigone's brother derives not so much from this requirement as from a most rigid view of the imperatives of regal authority, and from the overriding impulse not to be dominated by a woman. Consider in the context of these characterizations, the following statements of both Antigone and her uncle, Creon—first, illustrations of Antigone's love of family honor, and fascination with death:

Antigone. It's not for him to keep me from my own.

And yet what greater glory could I have than giving my own brother funeral.

For me, the doer, death is best
Friend shall I lie with him, yes friend with friend.
My life died long ago. And that has made me fit to help the dead.[25]

And, on Creon's view of the state, a ruler's authority, a subject's obligations, and women:

Creon. You cannot learn of any man the soul, the mind and intent until he shows his practice of the government and law.

Who counts another greater than his own fatherland, I put him nowhere. . . only so can we have friends at all.

The man the state has put in place must have obedient hearing to his least command when it's right, and even when it's not.

No woman rules me while I live.[26]

In the end, as is well-known, neither character will bend; both offend the gods in different ways. Creon confuses "the upper and lower world," sending Antigone living to the tomb, having refused burial to her dead brother; Antigone loses her life through her tempestuousness; and Creon loses his wife and son (Antigone's betrothed) through their suicides. Yet, the interesting points for our analysis lie in the play's exploration of differences between family and city (or state) and what is appropriate behavior in each.

Sophocles' two major characters are inverted images of one another—Antigone's complete devotion to family (and its honor in death) mirrored by Creon's equally complete devotion to the city and his own authority within it. What each could have learned from the other would have made good politics (and boring theater). That is, Creon confuses (or conflates) rule of the city and rule of the family, treating his subjects as though they were his children, and his wife and children as though they were only his subjects. In brief, he attempts to rule the self-sufficient association, the city-state, in abstraction from the chain of human ties that temper rule and make it humane, giving ballast to political abstractions like justice and honor by linking them to the ties of affection first learned in families. In the end, Creon is taught the importance of his own family, by having it taken from him. Antigone, by contrast, makes loyalty to family honor (her brother's burial) her overriding concern. (In this case she has the gods on her side, but it probably would have made no difference to her even if not.) She makes no attempt at a judicious balance between her family's honor and the requirements of the city-state, and, in the end, the error which brings her into being—the misguided attempt at familial self-sufficiency—is the cause of her demise as well.

The lesson in civic education for the audience within modern democracy (and modern scientific civilization) is in the insight—if it comes—that what is appropriate in one context is not directly so in the other, but that understandings gained in the experience of family life make flexible and livable the more abstract and general context—the state and its laws. If I am correct that one of the major dangers for the citizen of modern scientific civilization is the reductivist tendency to see all individuals, actions, and events as *qualitatively* similar instances of a law or "function," the *Antigone* performs a useful civic function for us not (following Aristotle's *Poetics*) by evoking fear and pity which lead to deliberation on the part of moderate citizens,[27] but by directing dramatic attention to the irreducibility of the city (or state) to the family and its concerns. This theme is treated in more expansive terms in *The Oresteian Trilogy* of Aeschylus.

The Oresteian Trilogy

The three plays of Aeschylus' tragic account of the close of the Trojan War and the growth of Athens were written a generation before Sophocles' *Antigone*. They deal with similar, but grander, more primitive, and more comprehensive themes associated with the founding of cities and the beginnings of political justice. In addition to the theme of the tension between houschold and city, female and male, they also treat the tension between old and new gods, between gods and humans, between older and newer forms of justice, and between force and persuasion in obtaining justice. The importance of the plays for our purposes, resides not so much in fine points of character (there are none developed besides those of Queen Clytemnestra) but rather in the general structure and outline of events involving general character types.

In this trilogy *(Agamemnon, The Libation Bearers,* and *The Eumenides),* Aeschylus reconstructs the inherited myths of Athens to tell a story about the emergence of legal justice and political persuasion from the blood feuds of a cursed royal family, against the backdrop of a conflict between newer Olympian gods (Apollo and Athene) and older, more primitive forces (the Furies). Here are the main characters and events. Upon returning to Argos victorious after a decade of fighting Troy, King Agamemnon is murdered by his queen, Clytemnestra (who is outraged at the sacrifice a decade before of their virgin daughger, Iphigenia, to obtain favorable winds), with the help of her lover, Aegisthus (who has an old score to settle with Agamemnon because of an older feud between their fathers). Cytemnestra is presented as a forceful, "manly," woman, outraged as well at what the decade of separation has done to her household ("that a woman should sit forlorn at home is a crying grief"[28]), and the preparer of an elaborate revenge. She first induces Agamemnon into a symbolic offense against Zeus, and then murders him in his ritual, cleansing bath, claiming divine justice on her side. "His death the work of my right hand, whose craftsmanship Justice acknowledges."[29] At this point, Clytemnestra is satisfied and calls for an end to the curse on the house of Atreus.

> *Clytemnestra.* Now to the Powers that persecute
> Our race I offer a sworn pact:
> With this harsh deed and bitter fact
> I am content; let *them* forget the past,
> Leave us forever, and oppress
> Some other house. . . .[30]

But the Chorus does not see the murder in the same light as Clytemnestra. At first unsure of where to place blame in this complex case ("Where, where lies Right? Reason despairs her powers"[31]), as *Agamemnon* ends, the Chorus calls for the return of Agamemnon's son Orestes to obtain justice for the murdered king.

> *Chorus.* Oh, does Orestes live? Kind Fortune, bring him home,
> To set against these two his sword invincible.[32]

The trilogy's second play, *The Libation Bearers*, opens years later with Agamemnon's son, Orestes, praying at his father's tomb for vengeance, a vengeance he himself subsequently delivers to both Aegisthus and Clytemnestra at the command (and threat) of the god Apollo, and at the urging of his sister, Electra. But this act of Orestes calls forth the wrath of the old, avenging Furies who punish acts against parents, hosts, and gods, and sets them against the newer god Apollo, who commanded Orestes to avenge the death of his father, and who watches over him. Just before his act of matricide, Orestes has an interesting exchange with his mother, Clytemnestra, which highlights the ambiguities of the drama's events with regard to justice.

> *Clytemnestra.* Your father sinned too. Count his sins along with mine.
> *Orestes.* Silence! He spent himself in battle, you sat at home.
> *Clytemnestra.* A woman without her man suffers no less, my son.
> *Orestes.* The man's work keeps and feeds the woman who sits at home.
> *Clytemnestra.* Are you resolved, my son, to murder your own mother?
> *Orestes.* It will be your own hand that strikes you dead, not mine.
> *Clytemnestra.* Beware the hounding Furies of a mother's curse.
> *Orestes.* How shall I escape my father's curse if I relent?[33]

The Eumenides, the last play of the trilogy, consists largely of dialogue and action among gods, although the outcome is a partnership with mortal Athenians instituted in a perpetual court (the Areopagus) sitting in judgment of future cases of homicide (an alternative not yet open to Orestes after the death of Agamemnon). In this play, Apollo, guarding Orestes from the avenging Furies, sends Orestes to the goddess of wisdom, Athene, who convenes a court of twelve mortals to hear testimony from Orestes, Apollo, and the Furies. (The Furies threaten vengeance on the city if they lose the case.) Apollo declares in his testimony that it was Zeus who gave him orders for the death of Clytemnestra and Aegisthus, because the Furies' old blood crimes are no longer more important than the life of a rightful ruler.

> *Apollo.* Zeus so ordained, and Zeus was right for their two deaths
> Are in no way to be compared. He was a king
> Wielding an honoured sceptre by divine command.[34]

And, after a split vote from the jury, Athene (a goddess born from Zeus' head rather than from a female's womb), also sides with Orestes, saying that his was the lesser crime.

> *Athene.* Therefore, a woman's death, who killed her husband, is, I judge, outweighed in grievousness by his.[35]

Then, employing the political means of "Holy Persuasion," and the threat of force (Zeus' thunderbolts), Athene manages to console, tame, and win over the Furies, transforming them from "blind" avengers into the more moderate Eumenides. Still, at the play's conclusion, they are to remain Fate's avengers, a necessary ingredient (in justice) to induce a moderate amount of awe and fear in citizens.

> *Athene.* Guard well and reverence that form of government
> Which will eschew alike licence and slavery;
> And from your polity do not wholly banish fear.
> For what man living, freed from fear, will still be just?[36]

Like Sophocles' *Antigone*, but even more so, Aeschylus' *Oresteia* gives content to the abstractions necessary for political existence, by showing dramatically how the abstractions became necessary for civilized life in the first place. In the case of the *Oresteia*, especially, this content appears as a series of tensions between opposites, which are held in balance in their healthy form, for instance, between household and city, between the old and new, between force and persuasion, and which create tragedy when disordered. Political justice appears as the moderate reconciliation of excessive claims on behalf of the extremes,[37] as in the case of the claims of Clytemnestra and Agamemnon, each of whom is prepared to destroy what the other loves, whether household or the city's glory; of the claims of Apollo and the Furies, neither of whom recognizes the essential importance of the ideas about justice of the other; and of Zeus and Athene (and the Athenian mortals) over the relative importance of force and persuasion in achieving justice. The final play of the the *Oresteia* implies, as well, that the escape from the cycle of blood vengeance lies in the distinctive, joint (immortals and mortals) achievement of established procedures of justice, calling for acts of objective judgment, which in their abstraction mitigate and elevate the more primitive passions leading to justice, without attempting to eliminate them completely.

From the standpoint of our theme about the reductivist tendencies of both democracy and modern science, the mythical events of these plays and their interpretation by Aeschylus, can lead the reader or spectator to see that *not only* may the recurring tensions which make up political existence not be eliminated without elimination of political existence itself, *but* that political and legal abstractions (concretely understood) were necessary historically for ascent out of the otherwise irresolvable conflicts of mere biologic and reproductive existence. Said differently, study and appreciation of the drama of the *Oresteia* teaches what it means to say (against the reductivist tendency of advanced democracy) that human existence at its most complete comprises formal (invisible, intellective) as well as substantive aspects; and it teaches (in the face of the "homogenizing" tendency of modern science and modern pluralism[38]) why the substantive aspects of political life may require dramatic and historical renderings if they are to be explained without being explained away.

Les Justes

The Aeschylean theme of the necessity for balance between the claims of primitive vengeance and urbane justice is further illuminated in a twentieth-century (1949) drama by Albert Camus, *Les justes*, or *The Just Assassins*. In this case, writing in a climate where political and legal abstractions had become the possessions of state bureaucracies and revolutionary intelligentsia, Camus is concerned about showing the dangers of (extreme) abstraction and formalism in the realm of political action, rather than their need (in the ascent from primitivism).

In this drama, set in Moscow at the beginning of the century (and based on an actual event), several young socialist revolutionaries plan and carry out the assassination of the Grand Duke Serge, by bombing his carriage. Most of the drama and dialogue is an exploration of the reasons for the use of lethal terror by the young revolutionaries; and also for their adamant refusal to repent the act afterward. All of them share the belief that terror is justified in order to free Russia and end a feudal tyranny which results in slow starvation for many of the poor. But, in the differing rationales of the various characters, Camus begins to raise questions about the nature and limits of "action" (to include terror) in a twentieth-century world of sufficiently complex organization and abstraction, that murder can be intellectually justified by any side.

The most barbaric (and woodenly abstract) character, and the one most likely to reproduce in a postrevolutionary world the evils that he set out to eliminate in the old one, is Stepan. He has been caught and tortured by the secret police, is driven by hatred, and sees the problem they face in "all-or-nothing" terms. And although he sees himself as an unromantic "realist," philosophically speaking, he is the most romantic of all in his drive toward the unconditional achievement of the group's goals in the realm of action.

Annenkov. I can't allow you to say that everything's permissable. Thousands of your brothers have died to make it known that everything is not allowed.
Stepan. Nothing that can serve our cause should be ruled out.[39]

And, again, on the same aspect of Stepan's character:

Stepan. Not until the day comes when we stop sentimentalizing . . . will the revolution triumph, and we be masters of the world.
Dora. When that day comes, the revolution will be loathed by the whole human race.
Stepan. What matter, if we love it enough to force our revolution on it; to rescue humanity from itself and its bondage.[40]

Yet another position on the justification for the use of terror comes from the young idealistic gentleman, Kaliayev, the character who actually throws (after one aborted attempt) the fatal bomb, and ascends the scaffold unrepentant. In his view, terror is necessary in order to achieve a new Russia, which will not only feed the poor, but will (without irony) resemble heaven on earth.

Kaliayev. A day will come when there's no more point in drinking, when nobody will feel ashamed, neither the fine gentleman, nor the poor devil who is down and out. We shall all be brothers and justice will make our hearts transparent. Do you know what I'm talking about?
Foka. Yes, The Kingdom of God, they call it.
Kaliayev. No, you're wrong there, brother. God can't do anything to help; justice is our concern.[41]

And, on his reasons for the assassination and his refusal to feel contrition:

Kaliayev. In dying, I shall keep the agreement I made with those I love, my brothers, who are thinking of me at this moment. And it would be betraying them to pray.
The Grand Duchess. One always dies alone. *He* died alone.
Kaliayev (Desparately.). No! No! One can die with them. Those who love each other must die together if they wish to be re-united.[42]

Some of Kaliayev's explicit understanding of the bond of love among the revolutionaries and its importance, would appear to come from the character, Dora, who clearly loved him, though without the opportunity to see romantic love grow. It is she more than any of the others who sees the necessary inhumanity of their personal existences for the sake of the revolution, and the necessity for personal redemption through love and loyalty to the group and its goals by death at the hands of the authorities.

> *Dora.* We don't belong to the world of men. We are the just ones. And outside there is warmth and light; but not for us. . . . Ah, pity on the just.[43]

And, after news reaches her that Kaliayev died unrepentant and dignified on the scaffold, remaining loyal to the group and its aims:

> *Dora.* Don't you realize this is the day of our justification . . . a sign for all the revolutionaries of the world. Yanek is a murderer no longer. A hideous crash! That was enough to plunge him back into the carefree day of childhood. . . . Yes, give me the bomb . . . next time, I want to throw it. . . .[44]

Now, where Camus stands on the events and dialogue of the play is difficult to know from the play itself, though not from his introductory remarks, which are quite explicit.

> It would be wrong to conclude that . . . in regard to the problem raised here, I recommend doing nothing. . . . I merely wanted to show that action itself had limits. There is no good and just action but what recognizes these limits and, if it must go beyond them, at least accepts death.[45]

And, on the general question of justice:

> Our world today . . . is made by men who grant themselves the right to go beyond those limits, and . . . to kill others without dying themselves. Thus it is that today justice serves as an alibi, throughout the world, for the assassins of all justice.[46]

These remarks, in combination with the dialogue of the drama itself, suggest that Camus is implying that radical action against large, complex, inhumane, state bureaucracies can guard itself from the similar, eventual inhumanity which it revolted against, by grounding itself in loyalty to small (natural?) groups, and by nourishing characters prepared to act at the expense of their own lives.

Whatever one may think of Camus's own romantic inclinations

here, *Les justes* is interesting for our purposes as a dramatic illustration of the potential excesses (and not necessarily those indicated by Camus) hidden in political and legal abstractions (e.g., justice) when detached from more primitive attachments. Read in conjunction, the *Oresteia* and *Les justes*, though pulling in opposite directions on the importance of political abstraction, are useful pedagogically in nurturing readers capable of attentiveness to both abstract and particular attachments;[47] who see the necessity for both in maintenance of a just, political equilibrium; and who have (at least classroom) practice in making the "intermediate" practical judgments necessary to link together the two (something the study of scientific generalizations can never do). On the general issue of the limits of all political action in the service of justice, I shall conclude this exploration with a brief look at one of Shakespeare's last plays, *The Tempest*.

The Tempest

Shakespeare's play *The Tempest* (1611), tells the story of what might be called an instance of "perfect justice," with every character receiving his due. But since this justice can only be dispensed with the aid of magical and supernatural arts, reading the play can begin to instill an appreciation of the inherent limits of political and legal justice, and in so doing, lay the basis for a reflective tolerance of the necessary diversity of human aims and endeavors in society and political society.

In this well-known play about a shipwrecked court on a strangely tropical island in the Mediterranean, a perfect justice is dispensed. A dukedom is returned to its rightful possessor, Prospero; two innocent young people find true love (Miranda and Ferdinand); usurpers are punished and made penitent (Antonio and Sebastian); a faithful spirit (Ariel) is freed of service to Prospero; a base, slavish monster, incapable of moral education (Caliban), remains a slave; and a basically honest, stoic individual (Gonzalo) is permitted to see justice done for his friend, though he himself remains largely unchanged. Yet the agents of this justice are for the most part magical arts acquired by Prospero, although there are other agents of justice as well, including the worthiness or baseness of the characters involved, their relative status in both the natural and civil order, and Fortune (or Shakespeare's art as the author of the play).

Much of Propsero's magical art appears to be based on the

ability to generate powerful illusions in the minds of those he wishes to influence.

Prospero. Say, my spirit,
How fares the King and's followers?
Ariel. All prisoners, sir . . .
They cannot budge till your release. The King,
His brother, and yours abide all three distracted. . . .
Your charm so strongly works 'em.[48]

Furthermore, once his aims are accomplished, Prospero vows to break his staff, drown his book, and "this rough magic . . . here abjure."[49] All of this, combined with the island setting, conveys the extraordinary nature of the complex and unusual justice meted out in the drama.

Prospero. Though with their high wrongs I am struck to th' quick,
Yet with my nobler reason 'gainst my fury
Do I take part. The rarer action is
In virtue than in vengeance. They being penitent,
The sole drift of my purpose doth extend
Not a frown further. Go, release them, Ariel.
My charms I'll break, their senses I'll restore,
And they shall be themselves.[50]

Moreover, Prospero is placed in the initial situation of having his dukedom stolen (we learn), precisely because he studied books to the exclusion of ruling men. The pedagogical effect on the reader is similar to that produced by a careful and complete reading of Plato's *Republic*—a growing appreciation of the practical impossibility of delivering through political institutions a justice which renders to each his complete due. And the intricate machinations (including the help of the spirit Ariel) necessary to accomplish the play's justice for each, also convey a sense of the complexity and difficulty of ruling in the service of so complete a justice, a lesson which both Creon and Dr. Stockmann might have done well to absorb. That is, to return to our theme, reading *The Tempest* can serve as a small antidote for the democratic tendencies to simplify and "homogenize" what each deserves, on the one hand, and to overestimate the capacity of political action to deliver even such an "homogenized" justice, on the other. (Consider John Rawls' *Theory of Justice* as a democratic "vision" guilty on both counts.[51])

There is another aspect of *The Tempest* which highlights another corrective in dramatic and poetic language (and theme) for the ailments of modern scientific and democratic civilization. This is that it deals with political and practical themes in poetic (and unpractical) images. The point is not simply that serious themes are sometimes best dealt with in the distance provided by poetic and aesthetic language, though *The Tempest* conveys this idea as well.

> *Prospero.* Our revels are now ended. These our actors,
> As I foretold you, were all spirits and
> Are melted into air, into thin air;
> And, like the baseless fabric of this vision,
> The cloud-capped towers, the gorgeous palaces. . . .
> Yea, all which it inherit, shall dissolve
> And, like this insubstantial pageant faded,
> Leave not a rack behind. We are such stuff
> as dreams are made on. . . .[52]

Rather, it is that a civilization whose dominant intellectual tendency is to explain phenomena (and human actions) by reducing them to instances or illustrations of general functions or laws of the quantification of nature, gains balance from sustained exposure to poetic and dramatic languages largely devoid of practical and quantitative symbolism.[53] And a civilization whose dominant political tendency is to equalize and homogenize its view of the diversity of human purposes (in the overriding interest of a uniform justice), also gains by sustained pedagogical exposure to dramatic writing done in advance of such reductivism. At the very least, languages are kept alive which permit appreciation of the potential complexity of human purposes, by the plausible depiction of such complexity in dramatic plot, dialogue, and confrontation—for example, of the kind evident in the various plays reviewed here.

Conclusion

Rather than simply summarize, I shall conclude by trying to say in general terms the role I see for classical and some modern drama in civic education for democracy. As I tried to show in the first essay of this book, democracy always generates the tendency to see what it is doing at a subpolitical level, that is, to conceive of its aims primarily in the context of subpolitical things such as families, homes, and personal appetites and desires. This tendency in all democracy to conceptualize political things in subpolitical terms is exacerbated in the case of modern American democracy by the emphasis on commerce; by the intellectual predominance of modern scientific modes of explanation;[54] by a millennialist cultural inheritance directed to the progressive elimination of the "political";[55] and by the passion for equality (depicted in detail by de Tocqueville) which compels us in the name of equal justice and winning electoral majorities, continuously to reduce our public languages to terms which will be meaningful to the simplest (and least political) of our citizens. Furthermore, even where modern democracy grasps the idea of the political as the context for other, subpolitical purposes, it is usually only to equate it with some substantive purpose such as exploiting more efficiently the resources of the earth, or bettering the physical living conditions of more and more people, or providing therapy for the alienation induced by such narrowly utilitarian purposes. The effect is, then, to make the political superfluous or exploitative—to lose sight of the political as the authoritative context for the pursuit of particular, substantive purposes and policies.[56]

But if these are the tendencies of our democracy, there is good reason to resist them in the hope of generating the kind of moral and psychological tension characteristic of the republican character described in this book's title essay. I have discussed the role of military service in this character formation in other essays; in this essay, I have tried to illustrate how drama may be used pedagogically as a corrective for the modern democratic and scientific predeliction to conceptualize in subpolitical terms. First, I have tried to show that drama illustrates, by putting things in perspective; by forcing the reader or spectator to grasp text and context throughout an entire story or plot (something scientific intelligence cannot do). And, secondly, I have tried to show how drama can be used to illustrate in detail, various consequences of employing subpolitical purposes for political ones, depending on the particular play being examined (and even where the playwright may have been hostile to the idea of the political). For example, as we have seen, *Antigone* and the *Oresteia* can be used to illustrate the relationship of the family to the city or state; *An Enemy of the People* and *Galileo* to illustrate the dangers of scientific reductionism of political things; and *The Tempest* and *Les justes* to illustrate the limits of political action in the service of justice.

Ancient and medieval legislators and writers tended to emphasize reliance upon the higher virtues and inclinations as correctives for the misdirection of political power for private gain and personal reputation. But we are inheritors of a different approach to political equilibrium, based in part on "enlightened" self-interest. A part of that "enlightenment" includes an analysis of the irrelevance (and potential tyranny) in using political terms and vocabulary to describe and justify subpolitical aims and interests; and a first step in that analysis (and for many people the only step) can be the study of drama to instill a detailed appreciation of the cultural losses entailed in reductivist social purposes and programs. In addition, and although it is outside the purview of this essay, one may perhaps hope that the pedagogical alliance of drama and political philosophy might dilute the iconoclastic and "deconstructionist" urges in contemporary literature and literary criticism, occasioned, in part, by (and in reaction to) the invasion of their realm by reductivist, ideological, and scientific ways of thinking about things.

1991–92

Notes

1. "The *Orestes* is on the verge of becoming part of the crisis it dramatizes, nearly a character in its own drama. This means an end to the separation of citizen-audience and stage actors, a separation that had afforded spectators a privileged position as knowing interpreters of action only partly understood by the characters on stage. . . ." J. Peter Euben, "Political Corruption in Euripides' *Orestes,*" in *Greek Tragedy and Political Theory,* edited by Euben (Berkeley: University of California Press, 1986), p. 247. Although Euben does not mention it, these remarks would apply in part to Jean-Paul Sartre's "subjectivist" rendering of the Oresteian story in *Les mouches.* And, in a circuitous fashion, Euben's remarks on Euripides' *Orestes* would apply to Eugene O'Neill's trilogy, *Mourning Becomes Electra,* which, while it preserves the judgmental distance between the spectator and the drama, is largely devoid of political or civic significance, that is, does not address spectators who also think and act as citizens. Still, neither Sartre's nor O'Neill's rendering of the Orestes story is as ostensibly aimless as that of Euripides, written during the (Athenian) chaos of the late (408 B.C.) Peloponnesian War.

2. "Further, no doctrine, so much as the Time-doctrine, lends itself to the purposes of the millennial politics of revolutionary human change, and endless 'Progress.' Nevertheless, we believe that the impulse to this doctrine is the outcome mainly of Science: that it is really the philosophy of the instruments of research. . . ." Wyndham Lewis, *Time and Western Man* (New York: Harcourt, Brace and Company, 1928), 434.

3. "The hypothesis . . . of Whitehead leads to the assumption of an equal

reality in everything, a democratically distributed reality as it were. . . . Time is *real*, and owing to this reality of time and change, it is we who are in the process of making a superior reality to ourselves: we are *mproving ourselves*. . . ." Lewis, *Time and Western Man*, 437. And, Lewis on Henri Bergson's views: "But, for a science that places all the moments of time in the same rank, that admits no essential moment . . . change is no longer a diminution of essence." (163) Lewis's view of time and change is clearly that of pagan, Athenian aristocracy, not that of the mixed republican character described in this book's title essay, but I cite it because it accurately describes the implications for time and reality of the modern scientific, experimental method.

4. The experimental psychology of Wundt and Watson, as transmitted to North American public school pedagogy through the influence of John Dewey, the education school of Columbia University, and sustained corporate funding, have had a more direct effect than the slower and more general one I am describing, in reducing the capacity for political and moral judgment in the average citizen of the United States. This thesis is expounded in detail in Paolo Lionni, *The Leipzig Connection: The Systematic Destruction of American Education* (Sheridan, Oreg.: Delphian Press, 1988), which argues that experimental psychology's view of human beings as *simply* the sum of their environmental experiences of pleasure and pain has led to a pedagogy emphasizing pleasurable and painful reinforcement in lieu of the practiced ability to make general judgments. "They have learned in school that what is pleasurable is good, and what isn't pleasurable isn't good. This is an inheritance from the stimulus-response teaching of Thorndike. . . ." (34) To fit this argument into my own thesis in this book, this development contributes to the formation of simplified, one-sided, democratic characters, impaired at making balanced judgments between the general good and their own good because unused to the idea that what is good may not be immediately pleasurable (i.e., a combination of likes and unlikes); and most certainly averse to maintaining the tensions of the republican character described in the title essay.

5. Even if the particular playwright in question had the most visionary and unpolitical purposes in mind—if he was writing for an audience that was still "political" in orientation, then in the skillful dramatist's work will be present some political understanding.

6. See, in this connection, n. 1.

7. Three of the plays analyzed here—Sophocles' *Antigone*, Ibsen's *Enemy of the People*, and Shakespeare's *Tempest*, have been a part of the introductory political theory course at Kenyon College for decades. For a description of this course, see Leslie and Charles Rubin, eds., *The Quest for Justice* (Needham Heights, Mass., 1987), 1–10.

8. Compare, for example, Ibsen's view of the relationship between truth, or openness, and politics in his play *The Pillars of the Community*, any edition.

9. Henrik Ibsen, *An Enemy of the People*, in *Four Major Plays*, vol. 2, translated by Rolf Fjelde (New York: Signet Books, 1970), 159.

10. Ibid., 127.

11. Ibid., 155.

12. Ibid., 197.

13. Ibid., 129.

14. Ibid., 190–95.

15. That is, more on the scientific side of "truth for its own sake." See Eric

Bentley, Introduction to Bertolt Brecht, *Galileo* (New York: Grove Press, 1966), 18–19.

16. Brecht, *Galileo*, 63.
17. Ibid., 64.
18. Ibid., 92.
19. Ibid., 77 and 79.
20. Ibid., 122.
21. Ibid., 124.
22. Ibid., 129.
23. Ibid., 124.
24. It is interesting to recall in this context that the complex city with a need for a military force, arises out the desire for more sophisticated pleasures in the dialogue between Socrates and Glaucon in Plato's *Republic*.
25. Sophocles, *Antigone*, in *Sophocles I*, edited by David Grene and Richard Latimore (Chicago: The University of Chicago Press, 1954), 161–62.
26. Ibid., 3 165–66, 177, 182.
27. For a development of this theme, see Stephen Salkever, "Tragedy and the Education of the Demos," in J. Peter Euben, *Greek Tragedy and Political Theory* edited by (Berkeley: University of California Press, 1986), 274–303.
28. Aeschylus, *The Oresteian Trilogy*, translated by Philip Vellacott (Baltimore, Md.: Penguin Books, 1956), 72.
29. Ibid., 91.
30. Ibid., 97.
31. Ibid., 95.
32. Ibid., 99.
33. Ibid., 137.
34. Ibid., 168.
35. Ibid., 172.
36. Ibid., 171.
37. For a development of this theme, see J. Peter Euben, "Justice and the Oresteia," *American Political Science Review* 76, no. 1 (March 1982), especially 27. "Like the heroic ethic, the life of the household and the dignity of those who sustain it are essential to a fully human life. . . . But the triumph of the *oikos* is as dangerous as the victory of the heroic ethic. This is because exclusive preoccupation with instinctive attachments . . . and biological life is too confining an ethic for living a fully just life. Its intensity precludes resolution of the dilemmas that it generates. . . . In the absence of reciprocity each goes to extremes and excess. . . ."
38. The emphasis on pluralism and toleration of "diversity" in modern democracy can be taken either as a recognition that the unchecked tendency of democracy is toward "homogeneity," or, more cynically, as a cover-up for the spread of this "homogeneity" of outlook. For a detailed account of an instance of this latter development, replete with dramatic irony, see David W. Lutz, "Can Notre Dame Be Saved?" *First Things*, no. 19 (January 1992): 35–40.
39. Albert Camus, *The Just Assassins*, in *Caligula and Three Other Plays*, translated by Stuart Gilbert (New York: Vintage Books, 1958), 257.
40. Camus, *The Just Assassins*, 256–57.
41. Ibid., 278.
42. Ibid., 289.
43. Ibid., 272.
44. Ibid., 301.

45. Ibid., x.
46. Ibid.
47. To clarify: overabstraction is the disease of formalistic science; particular attachment at the expense of all else, that of advanced democracy and tribal primitiveness. Abstraction grounded in a chain of loyalties and associations from the state to the family, is a condition for the healthy tensions I have associated with the republican character.
48. William Shakespeare, *The Tempest,* ed Robert Langbaum (New York: Signet Books, 1964), 109.
49. Ibid., 110.
50. Ibid., 109.
51. For a discussion of Rawls's views in this context, see the section on liberalism in the first essay of this book, "A Theory of Republican Character—For a Democratic Age."
52. Shakespeare, *The Tempest,* 103–4.
53. "In recent centuries the conversation . . . has become boring because it has been engrossed by two voices, the voice of practical activity and the voice of 'science'. . . . To rescue the conversation from the bog into which it has fallen . . . would require a philosophy more profound than anything I have to offer. . . . But there is another, more modest, undertaking which is perhaps worth pursuing. My proposal is to consider again the voice of poetry; to consider it as it speaks in the conversation." Michael Oakeshott, "The Voice of Poetry in the Conversation on Mankind," in *Rationalism in Politics and Other Essays* (London: Methuen & Co., Ltd., 1962), 202–203.
54. Scientific generalizations, again, are abstract about particulars, ultimately explaining them as quantitative illustrations of the physical properties of matter; whatever else, they are decidedly unsuited to the study of politics since (1) they possess no theory of prudence, that is, no theory about the application of their own theories, short of universal application or total abdication; and (2) they can only explain political phenomena by explaining them away, a tendency which the pedagogical use of drama (and the use of historical case studies) can be used to resist.
55. For the classic study of millennialist tendencies in North American politics, see Ernest Lee Tuveson, *Redeemer Nation: The Idea of America's Millennial Role* (Chicago: The University of Chicago Press, 1968).
56. For an expanded discussion of this theme, see the second essay of this book, "Some Correspondences Between Oakeshott's 'Civil Condition' and the Republican Tradition."

Epilogue

A brief Epilogue is in order owing to the ostensibly disparate subject-matters of the various selections in this collection. It also affords the opportunity to try one's hand—along with so many other hands of late[1]—at (an at least oblique) diagnosis of the *malaise* of American democracy and liberal democracy generally, right at the moment that it appears so successful on the "world scene."

My central theme has been about the tendency of advanced or old democracy to produce a kind of specialized character averse to, and largely incapable of, thinking and acting with consistency from a self-understanding which evaluates specific needs, wants, and claims on their own terms *as well as for* their likely effects on the broad political and constitutional arrangements which make their long-term satisfaction possible. Such democratic characters may contribute to the economic and technological vitality of a body politic, but they understand little of its political health and tend over time, as their social, pedagogical, and legal influence spreads, to render its political vocabulary superfluous by employing it to describe "subpolitical" activities associated with bodily and lower psychic needs; and insofar as they are capable of thinking about the "long term," it is primarily in terms of economic and psychological securities.

In Platonic terms, this is to say that democracy is the regime of the body and its needs,[2] and tends over time to produce characters who experience the world as a bequeather or withholder of increments of pleasure and pain, without much symbolic mediation or individual judgment in between, and without much inkling of experience transcending their environment of immanent pleasure and pain.[3] Said differently, the impulse of democracy (if left unchecked) is toward displacement of the political by psychology and economics, that is, toward elevation to the highest priority of personal happiness, understood and defined in the most reductivist psychological, physiological, and material terms.

Alexis de Tocqueville and Lockean liberals in America had

hopes that religion and its aversion to immediate gratification (as well as the understanding of the tie to a common Creator) might serve as a counter weight to the tendency of liberal democracy to nurture a kind of widespread, selfish "individualism." But, as we have observed, by separating politics from religion, and by removing religion from public education, the Lockean project provides in this instance no homeostatic corrective to the growth of atheism, pantheism,[4] and immanentist and scientific philosophies, that is, no political corrective for the loss of its own political and civic balance as its citizens grow more "democratic."

I have tried to suggest in the essays of this collection, that there are at least two inherited resources still at our disposal for regaining and retaining civic balance in this situation, that is, for nurturing the republican generalist outlook within an "immanentist" liberal democracy. One is service in a military system which views the use of armed force in the context of preserving a system of political authority, rather than in the context of a bargaining arrangement over increments of pain inflicted or withheld. The other is liberal arts education which employs (among other things) classical and other drama pedagogically to foster in students (and future citizens) a general orientation capable of viewing human society as a diverse mixture of "likes and unlikes," and thus makes available and familiar a mode of explanation which can serve as an *alternative* to the exclusive employment of scientific laws and metaphors about homogeneous human subject matter seen as illustrations of mathematical functions. In a subsequent volume, I investigate the historic role of the art of statesmanship in shaping modern liberal democracy, and its resources for mollifying democracy's more politically deleterious aspects.[5]

1992

Notes

1. One of the most salutary of this genre is Thomas L. Pangle, *The Ennobling of Democracy: The Challenge of the Postmodern Era* (Baltimore, Md.: The Johns Hopkins University Press, 1992). Still, it is curious that Pangle's hopes rest on the civic reeducation of a "postmodern" intelligentsia through exposure to the properly interpreted teachings of the apolitical Platonic Socrates.

2. This is my understanding of one of the themes of Plato's *Republic*, Books

7 and 8. See, also, Leo Strauss, *The City and Man* (Chicago: The University of Chicago Press, 1964), 109–15.

3. Apropos of this point is Pangle's quotation from a Christopher Lasch column on the "young people in our society," who "experience the world only as a source of pleasure and pain. The culture at their disposal provides so little help in ordering the world that experience comes to them in the form merely of direct stimulation and deprivation. . . ." Pangle, *Ennobling of Democracy* 80. For an attempt to demonstrate that this development is largely owing to the importation into American public school pedagogy of the experimental psychology of Wundt and Watson, by way of the education school of Columbia University (and sustained corporate funding for almost a century), see Paolo Lionni, *The Leipzig Connection: The Systematic Destruction of American Education* (Sheridan, Ore.: Delphian Press, 1988).

4. For a discussion of de Tocqueville's analysis of the tendency toward pantheism (that is, elimination of the "elitist" distinction between Creator and created) in democracy, see Peter Augustine Lawler, "Democracy and Pantheism," in *Interpreting de Tocqueville's Democracy in America*, edited by Ken Masugi (Savage, Md.: Rowman & Littlefield Publishers, Inc., 1991), 96–120. On de Tocqueville's view of Christianity's capacities for mollifying democratic materialism, see Ralph Hancock, "The Uses and Hazards of Christianity in de Tocqueville's Attempt to Save Democratic Souls," in *Interpreting de Tocqueville's Democracy in America*, 348–98.

5. The working title of this volume is *Statesmanship: Six Modern Illustrations of a Modified Ancient Ideal.*

Appendix A
"Two Views of Aristotle's *Politics*"

Rather than take on directly the rather broad topic I have been assigned ("Politics, Ancient and Modern"), I propose instead, and with your permission, to approach that subject more obliquely this evening, and in a way more consonant with my academic field of political theory. I propose to look at the first systematic treatise (lecture notes, actually) ever written on politics—the *Politics* of the fourth-century B.C. Greek philosopher, Aristotle. This work has been very influential in Western European political and intellectual life since its rediscovery and translation into Latin in the thirteenth century A.D. I shall look at it from two viewpoints, polishing each up to the best of my ability, and, then in respect for the complexity of the issues involved here, offer no definitive resolution of the conflict involved here, but rather a suggestion or two about how these two views might coexist in an uneasy tension with one another.

The first view is that Aristotle's basic outlook in the *Politics* is still basically sound and applicable to the modern world, with a few adjustments; the second is that its historical and cultural context is so different from our own as to make the *Politics* of largely historical significance, only. To make all of this interesting to an American audience imbued with the adversarial legal approach, I'll present the issues in such a way that you may use your own judgment on each as we go along. That is, I intend simply to take several observations of Aristotle from the *Politics* and the *Ethics*, and examine them from the standpoint of our two perspectives, which for the sake of your added enjoyment, I shall now transform into the two dramatic characters, "political theorist," and "historian."

First Statement (*Politics*, 1, 1, 2)

The most sovereign and inclusive (human) association is the *polis*, as it is called, or the political association . . . (we see) that the *polis* belongs to the class of things that exist by nature, and that man is by nature an animal intended to live in a polis.[1]

Historian. Aristotle wrote from the perspective of a system of small, often warring city-states, which even when they were democratic city-states, had more control over the habits of citizens and non-citizens than we are accustomed to in modern liberal democracy, especially in ethics and religion. But the modern liberal separation of church and state, the vast size and diversity of modern states, and the independence and cross-national interdependence created by modern technology and commercial practices, make the claim that the political association or state is the most "sovereign and inclusive" so laden with exceptions as to be no longer accurate in its essentials. Furthermore, Aristotle's claim that certain things exist "by nature"—when applied to activities of higher civilization and culture—is meaningless. We now know that once we are released by technology from the bonds of natural necessity, and unrestricted by oppressive political directives, the channels which human beings may seek for self-expression are so diverse, creative, and even idiosyncratic, as to make claims about what is "by nature" simply wrong, or, at best, too vague to be meaningful.

Political Theorist. "Aristotle claims that human beings are by nature beings made to live and participate in "*polis*-life," or life in cities of several thousands of citizens. He also tells us that the "nature" of any being is known by observing what it can become under the best conditions of growth, *not* what it is at its beginning, *nor* under average conditions. Thus, his claim would seem to be that human beings have the best chance of realizing their potential as rational or reasoning beings when they live in groups large enough to achieve economic self-sufficiency and military security, but small enough that all may have first-hand knowledge of others, and see clearly the consequences of their actions within the community—and make judgments about the regulation of their lives together based on these first-hand observation.

Surely, this is not a strange claim. Even in the United States of America today, one could hear a similar viewpoint from members of small towns (or other small communities such as liberal arts colleges) across the country in their criticisms of large cities, bureaucracies, and economic entities which "de-humanize" us by foreclosing knowledge of the consequences of our actions, or preventing our knowing (by their very size) whether we have "made a difference," or what the difference was. And this insight (which Aristotle makes) was surely in the minds of the founders of our government when they set up a *federal* system to incorporate the advantages of smallness with some of the military and economic advantages of largeness.

Aristotle's claim that the political association—or state as we call it—is the most sovereign and inclusive is also hardly strange to our ears. As a practical matter, what social, religious, or commercial entities could thrive without it in the face of competition of states, and their rights, privileges and powers? Where we would probably differ with Aristotle is in the claim that the political good is the most sovereign good, the one which includes and has priority over the goods and purposes of subordinate entities. We have inherited a religious tradition (now largely secularized) which points to paths of individual fulfillment and redemption detached from political considerations. But, closer inspection will show that the differences with Aristotle are not so vast as they may at first appear. To begin with, from a theoretical standpoint, both Aristotle and his teacher Plato held that the highest life, the philosophic and contemplative one, did not in any essential way require political participation. Second, from a practical standpoint, and in spite of our denials, political considerations do tend in the long run to "over-ride" or take priority over other considerations—military, economic, even religious—even for us in the "modern" world. (Consider our restrained tactics in limited warfare as an example of the first; the problems created by political borders for the laws of price-theory economics as an illustration of the second; and the increasing secularization of *all* aspects of American life in the interest of "social harmony" as an example of the third consideration.)

Second Statement (*Nichomachean Ethics,* 1, 2)

The art which is most of a master-art. Now, politics appears to be of this nature. In the first place, it is politics that determines what other arts should be studied, (by whom) and (to what extent) . . . and in the second place . . . the highly esteemed arts . . . of war, of household management, or oratory . . . come under the control of politics. If politics thus makes use of the other sciences . . . then the end of politics will embrace the ends of other arts and sciences. . . .[2]

Historian. Aristotle's claim that politics is the master-art, like his claim that political association is the most sovereign, will simply not hold in a meaningful way for the modern world. For example, the idea that politics regulates the other arts or decides which arts will be studied looks weak against the claims of the market and market forces to decide these questions in pluralist societies. And, issues not decided by market forces are usually decided by the requirements of advanced science and technology, or possibly in the Islamic world, by religious considerations. It has only been in the communist countries of Eastern Europe and Asia that Aristotle's claim for politics might carry some weight, and the events of the recent past show that even they are proving unable to resist the dynamic of supply and demand in the marketplace. Perhaps only in the realm of what might be called necessity—for example, the areas of defense and medical and environmental emergency—do politics and governance still qualify for Aristotle's rubric of master-art.

Political Theorist. It is certainly true that in modern pluralist societies the powers of the political and governing arts to regulate, are most direct and least ambiguous in the area of what we might call "necessity"—defense, basic security and welfare, and so on. But in a more indirect—yet still meaningful and important—way, politics and government can still be seen as the master arts. For example, liberal societies of the past two centuries have generally tried to exclude the realms of religion and economics from direct political control, but were these decisions not originally political? That is, were they not agreed upon in political processes and codified in political documents such as the Constitution of 1787? (And would these arrangements have endured without these political and legal supports?) Furthermore, in spite of these safeguards, doesn't politics, by way of government, still influence the fate of other arts and sciences? If, for example, capital gains taxes increase, what happens to stock market trading? If the Cambridge city council places restrictions on genetic experimentation within its borders, what happens to DNA research at Harvard? If the defense department, following Presidential and Congressional leadership, cuts back on weapons systems supported by major industries in Connecticut, what happens to the state's economy, at least in the short-run? And so on. Not only is Aristotle's observation still broadly accurate (if viewed with perspective) for large, modern liberal polities, but we can see as well that the most successful national political leaders are those able to grasp the Aristotelian idea that the state is not simply a big store, a big army, or big school, or big church, but all of these and more; and who see that the business of politics is to "prioritize" their respective claims for resources and legal liberties from the standpoint of the justice and welfare of the whole country.

Third Statement (*Politics,* 3)

Thus, it is clear that any state that is truly so called . . . must pay attention to virtue; for otherwise the community becomes merely an alliance . . . (where) the law is (simply) a covenant . . . and not designed to make citizens virtuous and just. . . . It is manifest therefore that a state is not merely the sharing of a common locality for the purpose of preventing mutual injury and exchanging goods. These are necessary preconditions of a state's existence . . . but a state is a partnership . . . in living well . . . produced by a feeling of friendship . . . and existing for the sake of noble actions, not merely for living in common.[3]

Historian. This last paragraph from Aristotle is a clear case of irrelevance for modern liberal democracies, generally viewed as the outcome of an implied social contract delimiting the role of government in especially religion, family life, and economics. In fact, most modern democracies would appear to be exactly what Aristotle says a state is not—a sharing of a common locality, with the laws viewed as a kind of contract or covenant for the purpose of preventing mutual injury and exchanging goods. Consider the views of John Locke, the seventeenth century English philosopher often viewed as the "theoretical father" of classical liberalism:

> Political power . . . I take to be a right of making laws with penalties of death, and . . . all less penalties for the regulating and preserving of property . . . and of employing the force of the community in execution of such laws, and in defense of the commonwealth from foreign injury. . . .[4]

> The great and chief end, therefore, of men's uniting into commonwealths and putting themselves under government, is the preservation of their property (i.e., lives, liberties and estates).[5]

And, furthermore, the foremost critic of this view of the purpose of political life, Karl Marx, proposed to overcome it by abolishing the state and all political life, a possibility he mistakenly thought realizable through the putatively huge economic surpluses to be generated by modern industry and technology. So it would seem that of the three statements from Aristotle thusfar, this last one—that the state exists to inculcate the higher virtues—is the least relevant to the modern, secular world.

Political Theorist. It would appear that on this point—the purpose of the state and politics—my historian friend has made his strongest case, and in the end, I may be inclined to agree with him, at least qualifiedly. But, before conceding too readily, let me offer several ways of viewing this matter which make his case less clear. To begin with, rather than say that the difference here is one between ancient and modern views, we might simply say that seventeenth (and eighteenth) century theorists like John Locke, took their bearings from ancient Roman theory rather than Greek. Consider, for example, these thoughts from the Roman republican, Cicero, writing about the middle of the first century, B.C., in his essay *On Duties:*

> For the chief purpose of the establishment of the constitutional state and the republic was that individual property rights might be secured. . . . For it is the peculiar function of the state and city to guarantee to each the free and undisturbed control of his own particular property.[6]

Or, to search for ambiguity on this point in the thought of Aristotle himself, consider that although he does say that in theory the state exists for the sake of the higher virtues, in his role as political scientist he goes on to describe what he considers to be the best regime in most circumstances—a "mixed" constitution combining parts from mass democracy and elitist oligarchy to produce a constitution favoring, and supported by, the commercial, middling classes, and achieving none of the higher virtues, moral and intellectual, with the possible exception of prudence in some leaders. (But aiming, instead, at simple stability, compromise among classes, and moderation in vices.) And, to quarrel with my colleague from the modern side of the issue, I might note that Locke was not the only modern theorist with something to say here. Other modern writers such as Montesquieu and de Tocqueville characterized modern liberal democracies as also existing for the inculcation of moral habits (not merely the protection of property), i.e., those habits of the commercial, middling classes which build their constitutions (and their lives) not so much on noble ideals as on mutual, countervailing and over-lapping self-interest.

Fourth Statement (*Politics*, 3, 6; 5, 1)

A constitution . . . the organization of a polis . . . especially in respect of that particular office which is sovereign. . . . In democratic states, for example, the people is sovereign, in oligarchies . . . the few have that position. . . . Both democracy and oligarchy are based on a sort of justice, but both fall short of absolute justice. . . . Democracy arose in the . . . opinion that those who were equal in any one respect were equal absolutely, and in all respects. . . . Oligarchy . . . arose from an opinion that those who were unequal in some one respect were altogether unequal (superior).[7]

Historian. These statements from Aristotle's *Politics* are illustrative of a view of politics which, again, is so comprehensive as to be largely irrelevant to modern liberal democracies, and even those authoritarian systems attempting of late to become like them. In brief, Aristotle is saying here that politics is about competing claims to rule other citizens, and to re-make those citizens in the image of the sovereign class, i.e., that the democrats try to mold all citizens into democrats, the oligarchs into oligarchs, and so on. Now, while we may have a pale image of this kind of robust and turbulent politics in our political parties, the scope of their claims on one another is much narrower, and also occurs within a constitutional framework which does not normally change with changes in partisan administration. Furthermore, as Tocqueville was already observing in the 1830s, all serious claims to legitimacy must now be based on the sovereignty of the people, or what Aristotle calls "the many." And, at least Anglo-American liberalism reached this greatly reduced and more stable brand of politics in reaction to a period of religious civil wars, and in a turning away from the view that the fundamental human activities should be to form, rule or conquer others. That is, modern liberalism embraced the view that the most fundamental *public* human activities were no longer political and theological, but rather economic and scientific, and directed toward conquering nature and scarcity rather than fellow human beings. (If you can read some French, you might like to see this theme developed in the chapter on John Locke in Pierre Manent's lucid little book, *Histoire intellectuel du liberalisme.*[8]) So, while Aristotle's statements are useful in gaining perspective on our own way of conducting politics, as a description of what occurs now, they are not very accurate.

Political Theorist. Here, again, my friend the historian makes some good points, especially with the idea that politics has been circumscribed in scope in the interest of avoiding strife over fundamental principles, as modern liberal societies have turned in the direction of ruling (destroying?) nature rather than ruling other men and women; as applied science and economics have become the important practical (non-military arts); and as ethical formation (or its absence) has become increasingly a private matter. Even here, however, Aristotle's insight (that politics is about competing claims to form other human beings) has direct relevance to our time, first in the cases of non-liberal, non-pluralist societies; and, secondly, in pointing us toward understanding one source of the tensions in modern liberal politics. That is, if Aristotle is correct that there is something abiding or permanent in human beings which leads them as general types—the warrior, the worker, the priest, the intellectual—to want to impose their view of justice on the others; and if modern politics is reduced to simply representing property or other substantive interests; then we can expect this ruling urge to erupt elsewhere. (For example, in schools, or churches, or in the streets, or in the unrestrained thoughts of thinkers like Friedrich Nietzsche, whose psychological reduction of theological and civil order became simply the infamous "will to power.") Even where we cannot return to Aristotle, we can use his insights as the basis for a political science capable of explaining better than can modern political science—because based on a more complete view of human beings—the tensions evident in modern politics and modern political history.

Conclusion

Rather than leave these issues between the political theorist and the historian wholly unresolved, let me (by way of concluding) attempt a statement of the more uncontroversial aspects of politics which can be abstracted from the theory and practice of over two millennia. Happily, I have attempted this before, and with your permission, shall simply read a concluding paragraph from an essay of mine entitled, "The Activity of Politics." In brief, the essay tries to find common elements between the practice of politics in Aristotle's mixed constitution and modern liberal democracy, both political systems sustained by the characteristics of the "middling" classes. Here is what I had to say in the conclusion to that essay:

> The picture of politics sketched here is that of an activity which moderately reconciles differences about policy among citizens or formal equal under general laws acknowledged to have legitimacy. It involves judgment, deliberation, artful persuasion, compromise, coercion, partisanship, and governance. Finally, although it may be abolished by something less free, politics is incapable of eliminating itself (as a basis for living together) in some "higher" freedom that transcends the "dualisms of existence." Politics, then, as a distinct human activity, has been viewed as the moderate or civil solution to living together. . . .[9]

For a final attempt at explaining in a simple and dramatic way some of the similarities and differences between ancient Greek and modern liberal outlooks on politics, I turn to some observations of the German poet, Johann Wolfgang von Goethe, on the drama of Shakespeare. I shall try in a moment to show the political relevance of Goethe's 1815 essay on Shakespeare, but first let me read to you some of his observations.

Goethe begins his brief essay by noting that the "predominant conflict in ancient literature is the one between moral obligation and its fulfillment, in modern literature between desire and fulfillment."[10] He then explains of ancient tragedy that

> it is based on an inescapable moral obligation which can only intensify and gain momentum if it clashes with an opposing desire. Essentially, this is where the frightfulness of the oracles resides, a domain where *Oedipus* reigns supreme.[11]

But, the modern world he characterizes this way:

> Desire is the god of modern times. Having become his worshippers, we are afraid of the opposing force, and this is why our art and our way of thinking will always remain distinct from the ancients. . . . Desire gave rise not to tragedy but to so-called drama, in which desire takes the place of awesome moral obligation.[12]

Goethe then goes on to place Shakespeare's work in the context of these two outlooks, by suggesting that Shakespeare sits uniquely between them.

> Shakespeare is indeed unique in that he fuses ancient and modern with such exuberance. In his plays, obligation and desire clearly try to counterbalance each other. . . . Many (of Shakespeare's) characters get into predicaments which they are not equipped to handle. Hamlet . . . because of the ghost, Macbeth because of the witches . . . and the superwitch, his wife. . . . Brutus because of his friends. . . . In short, we may say that the motif of desire that overpowers the individual is characteristically modern. *But since Shakespeare permits this desire to originate from without rather than from within, it becomes a type of obligation close to the ancients' concepts.*[13]

As a political theorist, I shall let others judge whether Goethe's is an accurate description of the differences between Sophocles and Shakespeare, and between Shakespeare and modern drama. But, broadly speaking, Goethe's account of the differences between ancient and modern, and of Shakespeare's attempt to bridge them, would approximate the efforts of the more influential of the classical liberal theorists—Locke, Adam Smith, and James Madison—who rather than try to dampen individual desire and appetite directly, sought rather to externalize and moderate it by channeling it into commerce rather than private tyranny, and into political institutions which pitted the desires and ambitions of some against those of others.

1990

Notes

This piece was delivered as an address to the International Studies Forum at Connecticut College, 7 March 1990.

1. *The Politics of Aristotle*, trans. Ernest Barker (London: Oxford University Press, 1946), 1 and 5.
2. Ibid., 354–55.
3. Aristotle, *The Politics*, trans. H. Rackham (The Loeb Classical Library; Cambridge: Harvard University Press, 1932), 215.
4. John Locke, *Two Treatises of Government*, ed. Peter Laslett (New York: Mentor Books and Cambridge University Press, 1960), 308.
5. Ibid., 395. (Parenthetic information added.)
6. Cicero, *De Officiis*, trans. Walter Miller (The Loeb Classical Library; Cambridge: Harvard University Press, 1913), 249.
7. Barker, *Politics of Aristotle*, 110 and 204.
8. Pierre Manent, *Histoire intellectuel du liberalisme* (Paris: Calmann Levy, 1987), especially 106. "L'économie, étroitement liée à la science, tend à devenit le lieu par excellence de l'activité humaine . . . parce que l'activité économique est . . . une action dirigée vers la nature et non vers d'autres hommes."
9. Wendell John Coats, Jr., *The Activity of Politics and Related Essays* (Selinsgrove, Penn.: Susquehanna University Press, 1989), 24.
10. Johann Wolfgang von Goethe, "Shakespeare Once Again," in *Essays on Art and Literature*, edited by John Geary (New York: Suhrkamp Publishers, 1986), 169.
11. Ibid., 170.
12. Ibid.
13. Ibid., 170–71. (Emphasis added.)

Appendix B
Review of *The Voice of Liberal Learning: Michael Oakeshott on Education*

> At least an institution like a University has a positive power of defending itself, if it will use it.
>
> —Oakeshott, 1947

Several recent favorable reviews of Michael Oakeshott's *Voice of Liberal Learning* have emphasized the impractical side of his views on teaching, learning, and places set aside for learning. What emerges from these journalistic reviews (*The Times Literary Supplement, Wall Street Journal,* and the *Economist*) is a view of liberal education as an initiation into a civilized conversation in which what is acquired are habits of self-enactment and self-disclosure within general practices and moral "languages." All of this is seen to be without any particular "vocational" value, but rather something prized for its beauty over its utility. There is certainly this aspect to Oakeshott's collected essays on education (written as lectures between 1949 and 1975), but if this were all he had said, most practical American readers might be excused for not being curious to know more about Oakeshott's views on teaching and learning than these reviews had digested for them.

But Oakeshott is saying more than this, and it is of practical (though not "vocational") significance. When the six essays of this volume (collected and edited by Timothy Fuller, Yale University Press, 1989) are read in the light of Oakeshott's comprehensive outlook, a considerably different emphasis can be discerned alongside of the one characterized in the reviews mentioned. To begin with, the impression that for Oakeshott a conversation is the appropriate image for the relationship of teachers and learners can imply an excessive relativism if taken out of context. A conversation is Oakeshott's image for the relationship among settled patterns of activity and thought ("modes"), such as history, science, poetry, and practice, because he is led by his philosophical skepticism to the view that there is no common standard by which these "voices" can evaluate one another's claims. But within any of these paradigms of thought and action, there is room aplenty for showing the error, absurdity, and irrelevance of most of what is thought and written. Oakeshott is quite prepared, for example, to convict most of what passes for philosophy, of irrelevance for venturing *directly* into the practical world.

The basis for this critique, both in philosophy and other areas, is a consistent viewpoint about experience, knowledge, and skill, which Oakeshott has asserted for decades in his various writings (especially those critical of "modern Rationalism"). This viewpoint occurs explicitly in this volume in the essay entitled "Learning and Teaching," as the claim that "knowing *how*" to do something, that is, questions of judgment and timing, cannot be divorced from "knowing *what*" to do, that is, specific actions to take. For Oakeshott, the form and content of all recognizable human activity arise simultaneously, and fluidly, and are inseparable except at the expense of lost skill and balnace. There are no *universal* methods or techniques (à la M.B.A. programs) which can be grafted onto inert, preexisting subject matters, because each new method creates its own subject matter in the way it "mediates experience" or organizes activity.

For Oakeshott, theoretical explanation is not a form of "doing," and cannot be equated with "doing" and retain its identity as a distinct human activity. Universities and schools, for Oakeshott, have traditionally been places of respite, released from the "deadliness of doing" in the interest of "explaining for its own sake." But explaining for its own sake has important consequences for practical activity in teaching us the limits of things, including theoretical reason. Consequently, to try to make liberal arts curricula "relevant" or "more practical," amounts to a categorical confusion of theory and practice, a reduction or contraction of our civilization, and a loss of historically acquired skills and judgments.

One quick but legitimate way of acquainting new readers with Oakeshott's general outlook is to compare and contrast it with that of Immanuel Kant. A common enterprise of the two is the attempt to rescue human freedom from the causal necessity of scientific laws. Kant's well-known solution in the *Critique of Practical Reason* is to show that we are free (or determine our own causality) when we conform our behavior to a conception of universal rules of morality. Oakeshott's truncated (and more Hegelian) version of this in "A Place of Learning" (and in *Our Human Conduct*, 1975) is that one is "free" by virtue of being a reflective consciousness which is what it has learned and understands (or misunderstands) itself to be, and which cannot be equated with "biological organism," "genetic character," "psychological ego," "economic actor," and so on. For Oakeshott, human beings are free not in willing the moral law, but in participating in inherited practices too general to define specific actions by themselves, and hence requiring acts of judgment ("knowing *how* to do something").

But, having cut itself off from Kant's account of a noumenal realm outside of time and space, Oakeshott's account is left simply with the assertion that what distinguishes human beings as beings capable of moral conduct is that they are what they learn to be, that is, what they make themselves in an understanding. Yet this would apply as well to a new breed of characters who have come to understand themselves predominantly in the languages and metaphors of biological, psychological, economic, genetic, and computer processes. They are simply the heirs of a very reduced inheritance—one of the obvious drawbacks of making liberal arts education "relevant."

Oakeshott's stronger suit lies not in this account of human freedom, but in his understanding of modern Rationalism, and his critique of it for the misguided belief that it can teach "universal" methods without disastrous practical and moral consequences. In order to make sense of Oakeshott's claim that the proper way to learn is in an apprenticeship which passes on the *how, what,* and *when* of concrete skills, it is necessary to refer to some of his other writings. To evaluate Oakeshott's claims from this side, the essays on liberal learning (especially "Political Education") must be read in conjunction with at least the title essay of *Rationalism in Politics and Other Essays* (London: Methuen and Co., Ltd., 1962), and the third essay, "The Tower of Babel."

In these essays, we are presented with an explicit view of each individual human mind as an historically evolved complex of inseparable methods and subject matters, and of the subordinate place of intellect in the moral practices of a balanced civilization, which to achieve balance must keep reason subordinate to unself-conscious traditions and rhythms—the generators of action in individuals and institutions. (Oakeshott's thought here provides a basis for criticism of imbalanced moral practices, and it is clearly misleading baldly to call him a "relativist," as some have done.)

Yet, the hallmark of these insights is not their originality (many of which Oakeshott attributes to ancient Chinese philosophy), but their lucid exposition by a master of the English language in the context of the past four centuries of Western intellectual and political life. For a generation of readers nurtured on "relevant" education, Oakeshott tries to make clear a fundamental derangement in the approach to knowledge adopted by "modern Rationalism"—"the most remarkable intellectual tradition of post-Renaissance Europe." I believe that it is in this context that Oakeshott's ideas about the inseparability of the *how* and *what* of learning in any concrete activity, will become interesting for modern American readers. (It is always fascinating to be shown one's origins.) Here is a practical side to Oakeshott's writing, a side intended to show to those who have eyes to see, what a grotesque reduction of the scope of human knowledge modern Rationalism has provided, and how this reduction grows more barbaric each generation, as it creates problems for which it claims to have the only solutions (more Rationalist problem solving), and steers formal education in the direction of that "relevance."

"Modern Rationalism" is Oakeshott's expression to describe a viewpoint, emanating from the vulgarization of some ideas of Bacon and Descartes, and characterized by a belief in the "sovereignty of techniques," applicable by almost anyone ("wits nearly on a level"), to almost any subject matter. In terms of our theme about the inseparability of the "how" and "what" of any concrete activity, the illusion of modern Rationalism is that it can capture or abstract the "how" of an actual activity and reduce it to propositions put in a book. But, in fact, it can never capture in propositions anything so "infected" with contingency as judgment or a sense of timing, and ends up by masquerading a part of the *what* or substance of a particular activity, in the guise of a universal or general method. When the use of abstract methods (themselves the distilled residue of some particular activity) results in loss of skill, the Rationalist compensates by retreating into an even more abstraction. (One example—not Oakeshott's—which comes to mind in this context, is the disastrous attempt by then secretary of defense, Robert McNamara, to use the management techniques of the Ford Motor Company to direct the Vietnam War; there is even a book-length account by Gregory Palmer using Oakeshott's categories of analysis to identify the confusions of the McNamara strategy.)

At a more general level, modern Rationalism's invasion of the realm of politics issues in the proliferation of abstract doctrines or ideologies directed toward the satisfaction of felt needs; and Rationalism's invasion of morality issues in forms of wooden and prosaic living by moral precept. Here we may without undue distortion abstract a practical interest from Oakeshott's view of universities and places of learning and wonder, rather than schools for vocational training. In an age in which the voice of practical interest dominates the "civilized" conversation, Oakeshott reminds us of other things. There is, first of all, the importance of theorizing for its own sake; there is its properly oblique relationship to the realm of practice; and there are also other voices like poetry which have neither practical nor philosophical concerns, on Oakeshott's view. Universities and schools can and should remind us of such things, but in order to continue to do so they must begin to defend themselves against the "Rationalist" onslaught—that is, universities and academies may have a practical interest without having a "vocational" interest.

If I follow Oakeshott's implication here, it is that universities and academies have something akin to an obligation to think clearly about the Rationalist invasion of their realm because the activity of problem-solving through sovereign techniques has no homeostatic or self-correcting capacities—it wants to do better but only knows how to become more abstract. Hence, universities, in order to defend themselves against such a perversion of their proper activity, must continue to pass on, in detail, civilization inheritances acquired before the rationalist seventeenth century. They will thus not only preserve their own patrimony, but help to maintain clarity about the abiding human things by (1) offering "full-bodied" alternatives for reflection to "selves" prone to self-understanding in terms of reductionist processes ("mine was the normal psychological reaction in the circumstances"), and by (2) making transparent in comparison the partiality and imbalance of enslaving knowledge to techniques in the exclusive service of felt needs and appetites. (But, of course, such insights are unattainable if, in lieu of studying them in detail, the civilizational experiences of, e.g., ancient Greece or medieval Europe, are thematically plundered for their "relevance" by the ideological disposition of the moment.)

In case I have been too abstract about all of this, let me try to say in a different way why these essays on learning and places of learning are important, and why they should be read alongside some of the essays of Oakeshott's book, *Rationalism in Politics.*

Here is a man as old as our century, with unusually refined historical and literary sensibilities, who has been watching carefully, and who, like others before and contemporaneously, is trying (obliquely) to tell us something about ourselves and the world we are making. This cannot be summarized in a sentence, but it has something to do with the fact that we (the literate of the race, at least) are slowly becoming rather simpler and less interesting beings than used to populate the planet, in our single-minded pursuit of practical and certain results, obviating much need for (what Kant called) reflective judgment. And, a corollary of this is that the prospects for reversal of this trend are even more dismal if places of learning cease being "places apart" and are drawn unaware into this project out of ignorance of their own historic distinctiveness. Other thinkers and artists have tried to convey this general idea as well, but it is the comprehensiveness, the coherence, and the gracefulness of Oakeshott's account which distinguish it.

Finally, a word or two on Tim Fuller's "Introduction." In placing Oakeshott's essays in the context of the current American debate over college curricula, Fuller distances Oakeshott from two prominent voices, those of E. D. Hirsch and Allan Bloom—the former for being part of the problem (i.e., plundering history for abstract solutions to "relevant" problems), and the latter both for viewing our educational dilemma as a political crisis, and for overestimating what philosophical thinkers can do about it. (Isn't the issue here really whether there are ever any abrupt, unmediated changes in the general ideas of a nation or civilization?) In Fuller's tableau, both writers are seen (not unfairly) to have lost their balance opposite the more detached and graceful Oakeshott.

Yet, as I have tried to show, while there is a "conversational" side to Oakeshott's writings, it is primarily as a postulate of intelligibility for relating the various modes of experience and disciplines of inquiry, rather than an attitude toward one's critics on a determinate subject. (In fact, Oakeshott's writings can be merciless toward those he considers bunglers—witness his treatment of the Moberly report in the essay, "The Universities.") Still, in the midst of the current shouting match over college curricula, Fuller is on solid ground highlighting the more Platonic aspects of Oakeshott's orientation. I have meant only to speak to readers whose attention was not yet engaged by the prospect of knowing more about what Oakeshott has to say.

1989

Index

Aeschylus: Orestian trilogy, 129–33
Aristotle: on mixed regime, 9, 16–19, 39, 53, 54n.5, 6, 12, and 13, 153; on politics, 147–57
Armed force: relationship to constitutional forms, 18, 20, 31, 39, 50–53, 145

Betts, Richard: on Vietnam war, 89–90
Blackstone, William: on self-defense, 52
Brecht, Bertolt: *Galileo*, 124–27
Brennan, William: ideas of, 41–43
Bundy, McGeorge: on Vietnam war, 105, 114n.40; on Cuban missile crisis, 113n.19
Burke, Edmund: ideas of, 40

Camus, Albert: *Les Justes*, 133–36
Cato's Letters, 33, 68
Character, democratic, 9–10, 16, 29, 36–43, 45, 51, 53, 64–66, 110, 119–21, 137–40
Character, republican, 9–11, 15, 29, 33, 36–43, 48, 53, 64–65, 139
Cicero: ideas of, 9, 20–21, 39, 152
Clausewitz, Karl von: on defense and war initiation, 96
Cooper, James Fenimore: on democracy, 31–32, 35, 47

Defense: political implications of, 112, 118n.95
Delbrueck, Hans: on attrition warfare, 81
Douhet, Guilio: on air power, 113n.8
Drama: pedagogic functions of in democracy, 140, 143n.54, 145; and republican character, 140, 155–57

Eidelberg, Paul: on mixed regime, 57n.75
Euben, J. Peter: on Euripides' *Orestes*, 140n.1; on political justice, 142n.37

Federalist Papers, 26–29, 33, 50, 116n.70
Ferguson, Adam: ideas of, 9, 39
Fuller, Timothy: on Michael Oakeshott, 163

Galen: ideas of, 15
Garthoff, Raymond: on Cuban missile crisis, 85
Gelb, Leslie: on Vietnam war, 89–90
Goethe, Johann Wolfgang von: on Shakespeare, 155–56
Grotius, Hugo von: on punitive war, 78
Gulf War, 10, 12n.5

Hamilton, Alexander: ideas of, 31, 50
Hannah, Norman: on Vietnam War, 86–88
Harrington, James: ideas of, 9, 23–24, 47
Hobbes, Thomas: on silences of laws, 67

Ibsen, Henrik: *An Enemy of the People*, 121–24

Kant, Immanuel: ideas of, 31, 74, 159–60, 162
Kennedy, John Fitzgerald: and Cuban missile crisis, 81–84, 145n.60

Lasch, Christopher: on modern youth, 146n.3

Lewis, Wyndham: on time-doctrine, 140nn. 2 and 3
Liberal Arts education, 159, 162
Liberalism, 10, 144–45, 151, 154; and republicanism, 43–50, 152, 155–57
Lionni, Paolo: on American education, 141n.4, 146n.3
Locke, John: ideas of, 44–45, 60n.110, 144–45, 151–52
Lowi, Theodore: ideas of, 59n.94

McCone, John: and Cuban missile crisis, 83–84, 92, 104, 111
McDonald, Forrest: ideas of, 27, 70
Machiavelli, Niccolo: ideas of, 9, 21–24, 56n.28
McNamara, Robert: ideas of, 10, 78–102, 111, 161
Madison, James: ideas of, 9, 27
Manent, Pierre: *Histoire intellectuele du liberalisme*, 154
Marx, Karl: ideas of, 55n.13, 152
Mass media: and democracy, 91–92, 104–8, 111
Meier, Christian: on Aristotle, 54n.5
Millennialism, 139
Mixed regime, 9, 16–20, 39, 75n.5, 153
Modern Science, 119–21, 132–33, 136, 138, 140–41n.3, 145, 152
Montesquieu, Baron: ideas of, 26, 69, 153

Nietzsche, Friedrich: ideas of, 155
Nitze, Paul: ideas on arms control, 109

Oakeshott, Michael: ideas of, 11, 43, 45–48, 60n.103, 63–77, 143n.53, 158–63
Ober, Josiah: on mixed regime, 55n.17, 75n.5

Pangle, Thomas: ideas of, 59n.92, 145n.1
Pantheism: and democracy, 145
Partisanship, 40
Plato: on democracy, 10, 54n.3, 110, 144; on justice, 73, 137; on foreign policy, 115–116n.60
Pocock, J. G. A.: ideas of, 23–24, 47, 58n.85, 64, 69, 71
Political: idea of the, 36, 42–43, 50, 55n.25, 72, 73, 132–33, 136, 138–40, 144–45
Polybius: ideas of, 20–21

Rationalism: Oakeshott on, 47–48, 72–73, 161
Rawls, John: ideas of, 44, 48–50, 137
Reagan administration; and use of force in Beirut, Grenada, and Libya, 100–104; arms control policies of, 108–9, 117n.87
Republicanism: ancient *vs.* modern, 10, 26, 43–50, 152
Robertson, John: on city-state militia, 61n.125
Roosevelt, Franklin D.: ideas of, 35–36
Rousseau, Jean-Jacques: ideas of, 24–26, 32, 74

Schelling, Thomas: on punitive use of force, 79–81, 90, 112n.3
Schultz, George: policies of, 101, 117n.89
Shakespeare, William: *The Tempest*, 136–38; Goethe on, 155–56
Socrates: ideas of, 54n.3
Sophocles: *Antigone*, 127–29
Stevens, John Paul: ideas of, 42–43
Stevenson, Adlai: ideas of, 40

Tarcov, Nathan: on John Locke, 44–45
Texas, Petitioner vs. Gregory Lee Johnson, 41–43
Thies, Wallace J.: on Vietnam War, 90–91
Thucydides: ideas of, 19
Time: and republican and democratic characters, 36–41, 58n.85, 58–59n.91
Tocqueville, Alexis de: ideas of, 9, 29–31, 49, 69, 110, 144–45, 146n.4, 153

Vietnam War, 10, 85–95
Voegelin, Eric: on progressivism and atheism, 58n.88

War Power Resolution of 1973, 101–2, 111
Webb, James: ideas of, 78
Weinberger, Casper: policies of, 103, 115n.59
Wilson, Woodrow: ideas of, 9, 32–35